Testimonials

'A must for any credit risk analyst starting out or as a point of reference when embarking on any analytical task. This clear, concise, comprehensive, and practical guide to credit risk analytics provides insights into what analysts take years to learn from others. It is so rare to find such an excellent and easy-to-understand introduction to the practical world of credit risk. I look forward to Carolyn's next book!'

Eva Neves, COO, ADEPT Decisions

'It's rare to find a book on credit risk that is so well written and easy to understand. I loved the way Carolyn sets out key concepts in such a lucid and attractive style, often drawing on her real-life experiences. She provides an expert view of the credit risk cycle, offering superb advice throughout. This book is a great introduction to credit risk. It will be invaluable for anyone new to the industry, as well as for more seasoned analysts looking to expand their knowledge base.'

Stuart Baxter, GM Analytics, Centrix

'My impression of *It's a Risky Business* fits a Chinese phrase 深入浅出|*shēn rù qiǎn chū*, that may be translated as 'in through the depths and shallows'. It is written by a mentor who has a deep grasp of complex subjects yet can convey them in simple terms. The plain, conversational tone of this book would be a great template for analysts to emulate when we collaborate with others. *It's a Risky Business* would be a perfect learning roadmap for developing analysts.'

Scott Liang, Head of Credit Risk NZ, humm group

'I found the book to be a very clear introduction with great progression into the more complicated aspects of credit risk.'

Michael Steele, Senior Credit Risk Analyst, Flexi Cards

It's a Risky Business

IT'S A RISKY BUSINESS

A field guide to Retail Consumer Credit Risk Analytics

CAROLYN RÖHM

Published by Carolyn Röhm

First published in 2022 in Auckland, New Zealand

Copyright © Carolyn Röhm

www.carolynrohm.com

Edited by Jenny Magee

Designed and typeset in Australia by BookPOD

Printed by Print House, Hamilton

ISBN: (paperback) 978-1-99-118470-2

ISBN: (ebook) 978-1-99-118471-9

This book is dedicated to Dieter, Michaela and Kaitlyn. Your ongoing confidence, encouragement and support mean the world to me.

Contents

Introduction

'It's a dangerous business, Frodo, going out your front door. You step onto the road, and if you don't keep your feet, there's no knowing where you might be swept off to.'

– Bilbo Baggins; JRR Tolkien, The Lord of the Rings

To be fair, you are unlikely to meet dragons, elves, hobbits or orcs in even the gnarliest retail consumer credit risk analytics. Still, unwary analysts may find themselves wandering off track, spending hours, even days, chasing shadows and not making progress.

This book is a field guide to retail consumer credit risk analytics and takes a first principles approach. I use the terminology generally found within credit risk, although I'm sure you can add language that is specific to your organisation or associated with areas adjacent to credit risk, such as diallers.

'First principles' means I've covered specific pieces of analytics that, once mastered, will serve you well as a credit risk analyst.

It's a Risky Business

I'm assuming you have a basic appreciation of how to open data in Excel or through code. I have specifically steered away from providing code snippets. Credit risk analytics can be performed by hand (although I really don't recommend it!). Whether you're an Excel whizz or prefer Python is immaterial to the actual analytics. Besides, you can google how to write code if you don't know, and there are plenty of learning opportunities.

My focus is on the principles of credit risk so that aspiring analysts learn the language of our profession and understand what we're talking about.

When learning new stuff, we have to unpack everything, lay it out, then sift through it and find what is relevant and useful. Once we know something, that long-winded process is no longer necessary. We seamlessly and effortlessly combine the necessary information to understand what we're looking at.

This book is for credit risk analysts at the start of their careers or with some experience under their belts. It provides a solid understanding of what we talk about and how everything hangs together.

In credit risk, nothing happens in isolation. It is overly simplistic to think that a change in account originations won't impact subsequent risk. That includes delinquencies, spend and interest revenue. These impact collections activities, which affect subsequent spend and so forth. All these things impact overall profitability and customer experience, but these relationships are not always obvious or immediate. Some actions can take months to manifest as repercussions.

This book will embed the core principles of retail consumer credit risk analytics, so analysts can make intuitive leaps, understand, analyse and recommend appropriate actions and identify opportunities.

The purpose of analytics is to drive change. Credit risk analytics is no different. When done well, credit risk analytics drives increased revenues by onboarding appropriate segments and increasing spend and interest earned. All without increasing the costs associated with increased delinquencies.

> **When done well, credit risk analytics drives increased revenues.**

When things go awry, as they sometimes do, credit risk analysts are the ones who dig into the detail and piece together the unexpected. We determine appropriate remedial actions and communicate them effectively. It's what we do.

By the end of this book, you will have a solid foundation of all things retail consumer credit risk related. From that point onwards, it is up to you to put the skills into practice. May the odds be ever in your favour!

What is retail consumer credit risk analytics?

Finding a definition of retail consumer credit risk analytics is a challenge.

While I firmly believe that Google is our friend, a Google search doesn't always yield particularly informative results. After a bunch of advertisements, there's a result from the Corporate Finance Institute that says, 'Credit risk analysis is a form of analysis performed by a credit analyst to determine a borrower's ability to meet their debt obligations.'[1]

In a nutshell, that's correct.

Retail consumer credit risk analysis is about consumers (not corporates or businesses) and involves credit within the retail space – retail banking, store credit, personal loans, credit cards, store finance etc. But retail consumer credit risk is about so much more than determining whether an individual can meet their debt obligations. That's more about affordability.

So, what is retail consumer credit risk analytics? And how do you recognise it?

I started work as a credit risk analyst in early 2000. Even after I was interviewed, offered and accepted the role, I had little idea of what I was getting into. It seemed interesting; I needed to be numerate and deal with some stats and maths. My new boss wasn't particularly concerned that I didn't have experience in credit risk; I had the necessary skills.

The company employed two of us as credit risk analysts. We worked in retail consumer credit risk (although I doubt either of us would have been able to articulate that then). My new colleague was an honours graduate in physics, and I was an honours grad in ocean and atmosphere science. Our boss was a chartered accountant (CA). Our similarities? We were all pretty handy numerically, and logical thinking was our strong suit.

We started by learning how to run the weekly and monthly reporting. One of our functions was to deliver reporting on performance to the wider business. What proportion of business, sliced in a multitude of ways, had reached the very important 90-days past due mark?

My new colleague and I had no idea what we didn't know, and from a credit risk point of view, there were many unknown unknowns.

Several months later, a new chief operating officer was appointed who did know a lot about credit risk. He quickly surmised that our (the full credit risk team) technical skills were not up to scratch. He brought in consultants who specialised in retail consumer credit risk. (That's all they do.) These two consultants did exactly what consultants do. They asked questions and produced a report. When I read that report, I realised there was so much I didn't know or understand.

Then, the consultants delivered a three-day offsite.

I consider those three days my true introduction to retail consumer credit risk analytics. The lead consultant patiently and carefully stepped us (the risk team, the originations team and the collections team) through their findings. It was remarkable and eye-opening.

They started at the beginning, with account originations, with credit assessment, policy rules and the use of credit bureau information. They walked us through the credit risk life cycle, what it is and how what we do at one point in the cycle impacts what happens at other points.

We discussed the use of recency instead of delinquency to assess whether accounts were in good order. We discussed the concepts of the minimum amount due and what constitutes a payment. We discussed collections activities and how those activities impact future spend on accounts that make payments. We discussed credit limit settings and whether they were appropriate. We discussed the theoretical breakeven odds at the point of originations and how our bad definition may impact that calculation. We discussed gross charge-off rules and the impact of those rules, combined with what constituted a payment, on the business's profitability. We discussed marketing activity and which customers we attracted. We also discussed marketing activity to existing customers and the impact of our risk settings on repeat purchases.

Retail consumer credit risk analytics is about all this and more. It includes understanding the credit cycle and its impact on the credit risk life cycle. It is about understanding how what we do at the point of account acquisition impacts operations in the underwriting and collections teams. It's about understanding how different products perform. Credit cards and personal loans are both retail consumer products, and identical rules can (and do) produce different outcomes and downstream impacts.

Why is retail consumer credit risk analytics important?

Now that we have a better idea of what it is, let's look at why it matters. Again, Google is our friend. According to the Corporate Finance Institute, credit risk analysis is important because it 'helps the lender determine the borrower's ability to meet debt obligations in order to cushion itself from loss of cash flows and reduce the severity of losses.'[2]

According to Graydon, credit risk is important so that lenders don't lose [too much] money.[3] Again, we see that the key reason for risk analytics is to ensure that losses are reduced, minimised or controlled. Yet while this is technically accurate, I find it far too narrow.

We perform credit risk analytics for several reasons, including minimising losses. I guess the easiest way to minimise losses is not to lend money. That would certainly meet the goal of minimising losses, as there wouldn't be any. However, there would not be any profit, and nor would there be a lending business.

So, let's consider why credit risk analysis is important. After all, we want it done well.

We perform credit risk analysis to understand where our losses come from and how they relate to other aspects of our business. We may have a product or a tranche of customers that, when viewed in isolation, have higher loss rates than are desirable. However, further investigation may highlight that those customers who don't become early losses can later become long-term high-value customers, offsetting the initial unfavourable and unpalatable loss rates.

Credit risk analytics ensures that we understand the impacts of various activities, at origination or during marketing campaigns or collections, on subsequent revenues and losses.

Credit risk analysis is not, or should not be, only about reducing losses. Yes, constraining or minimising losses are important, but they are only one part of the equation. Credit risk analysis helps us understand where revenues come from and optimise the risk/reward equation.

> **Credit risk analytics ensures that we understand the impacts of various activities.**

A common refrain in credit risk is that high-revenue customers are often high-risk and that low-risk customers are, inevitably and unfortunately, low-revenue customers. Broadly speaking, this maxim holds true.

However, some high-revenue customers are also low-risk. So, here's the first of many top tips: we want to be able to identify these people so we can encourage more of them to become customers. Similarly, there are low-revenue customers who happen to be high-risk. We do not want to encourage them to become customers!

Credit risk analysis is important as it ensures we can find the nuances. We want to identify what works well, delivers increased operational efficiencies and revenues, decreases losses, and do more of those. Similarly, credit risk analysis helps us identify what isn't as effective as we would like. Once we understand these areas of opportunity, we can determine and implement the best or most appropriate course of action.

Credit risk analytics also matters from an operational point of view. Within operations, front-line staff see things that analysts, with their large data volumes, do not. This means that front-line staff can highlight their concerns to analysts for deeper analysis to determine whether a change in approach is required.

This can be, and often is, a double-edged sword. Operations teams tend to see a subset of the applications or accounts. Typically, they're asked to underwrite the high-risk accounts at the origination point or determine whether to override an automated decline.

Similarly, in late-stage collections, the operations teams only see accounts that become seriously delinquent. This can lead to mistrust of the credit risk processes and the teams responsible for risk assessment, with team members calling out what they're concerned about.

As analysts, I urge you to listen to these concerns. Sometimes these teams identify nuggets of gold. They can identify small (but significant) clusters of applications or accounts. In doing so, we can quantify the risk these applications and accounts pose, determine the true scale of the opportunity, and recommend a way forward that reduces the risks and associated costs and increases the benefits and associated revenues. All this is why retail credit risk analytics is essential.

How to use this book

This book is structured so that each module can be viewed and understood in its own right. However, it would be unwise to launch into Module 4 until you understand the concepts outlined earlier.

Module 0 focuses on analytics basics. I expect most analysts already have a good understanding of the topics covered in this module. However, I have included it for those who have not formally been inducted into analytics and may have come across credit risk analytics through a different path.

Module 1 focuses on fundamental credit risk concepts. As an analyst new to credit risk, I felt like I had dropped into some weird alternative reality, where I could understand the individual words spoken, but the sentences didn't make sense. Module 1 unpacks the key concepts and terminology that is pervasive in retail consumer credit risk analytics.

Module 2 focuses on the core building blocks of credit risk analysis. These elements are useful in their own right and must be well understood.

Module 3 introduces the final concepts and building blocks. These are more complex and leverage learning from previous modules.

Once you understand all these concepts, the final step to mastery is to bring it all together appropriately using various skills to solve myriad complex and challenging issues.

I have tried to identify the core elements of retail credit risk analysis and break them into first principles. I firmly believe that once an analyst understands first principles, all problems, challenges and curve balls can be addressed.

Module 0

Analytics Basics

'The goal is to turn data into information and information into insight.'

– Carly Fiorina, former executive, president
and chair of Hewlett-Packard

There is absolutely no analysis without data. And depending on how and where we source data, a significant amount of work may be required for it to be used reliably.

In this module, we explore the basics of analytics:

- The importance of importing data and key considerations to bear in mind
- The power of exploratory data analysis and why it is critical to success
- What we mean by data validation
- Why ethics and data source reliability are important.

001: Importing data

Importing data is one of the most common processes an analyst undertakes.[4] Why do we do it? Importing data into a tool to analyse it and combine it with existing data enables us to perform analytics and add value to our teams and organisations.

Data comes in many forms. It could be scraped from a webpage or a static file (typically a CSV) downloaded from a source system. Most comes as a flat file, or is processed via an extract, transform and load (ETL) process into a data warehouse (DWH). With the deluge of available data and the reduction in storage costs, many organisations are now opting to extract and store data in data lakes, making it readily available to analytical teams. Before teams can use it or determine the best transformations so it can be loaded in the DWH, the data must first be imported, examined and understood.

> Many organisations are now opting to extract and store data in data lakes.

Importing data involves reading a file into a tool so it can be assessed, used or analysed. You will add considerable value to your team and organisation if you can do this and combine it with other data to produce valuable insights.

Flat files (CSV, TXT files, etc.) are typically read into the analyst's tool of choice through a wizard or an import statement. You can perform analytics in any tool you prefer. Excel, SAS, R and SQL are some of the common ones.

Considerations

Is numeric data always best imported as a number?

Sometimes it is helpful to think of numeric data as characters, for example, application numbers, account numbers, customer numbers or card numbers. These fields often contain leading zeros, so if you import your data as a number, those zeros will be lost. If you plan on matching your newly imported data with existing data, it is worth ensuring that your match keys are of the same type; otherwise it will likely fail.

Dates

Dates are wonderful things! Dates should definitely be imported as dates. Every analysis tool I have ever worked with enables date calculations. That means you can calculate the number of days between dates, ages, years or months. You can figure out the date X days before or after a specific date. That means you can create date or time-based variables based on date variables

Dates should definitely be imported as dates.

that already exist in your dataset. This is an extremely useful feature in credit risk analytics.

Headers

Does your data have headers? If it does, use the header record to assign names to each column. If not, you may want to assign a feature name to each variable.

Delimiters

Whilst CSV files are typically comma separated (as the name suggests), this is not always the case. If the file uses something other than a comma, this may need to be explicitly stated in the import wizard or the import statement.

002: Exploratory data analysis

Do not underestimate the power of exploratory data analysis or EDA. It will help you understand your data, even though, at first glance, it may seem dull and boring. Conducting EDA means you will become familiar with the data and gain insights that will add value.[5]

The primary purpose of EDA is to detect errors in your data and understand the patterns and shape of your data.[6] Once you have completed EDA, you will better understand your data. This will inform decisions around how the data can be used and clarify business decisions that impact the business's bottom line.

Analysts and data scientists use EDA to find patterns within the data and understand the underlying structures within data. They seek to understand how features are related, see the data, and detect anomalies or errors. Analysts will often chart or plot data to better visualise hidden patterns.

Once you understand your data, you can start extracting insights, which is where the value lies. Data is the raw ingredient; the value comes from understanding and using it to develop insights that help your team and company deliver increased value to customers.

Eye-ball the data

I like to see my data. I don't need to see it all, but I do like to check whether it has mostly been imported correctly.

A scan may reveal some fields have been imported as numerics, which would be better imported as string fields. You may also see that your date format needs tweaking – remember, dates should always be dates so that you can use them meaningfully in calculations.

Fields, data types, rows and columns

Once you're happy that your data has been read in correctly, it is time to develop an understanding of the data.

Printing the information associated with the data frame or dataset gives a list of all the columns, a count of the number of non-nulls for each column, and the field name and data type, including the index range.

By now, you should have a feel for the data – what the fields are, each field's data type, how many **null** (missing) values each field has, and the total number of rows and columns.

At this point, we can start looking at the fields to increase our understanding of the data.

Descriptive statistics and classification distributions

Descriptive statistics is a great place to start. It is where we look at individual variables in one dimension.[7] These are summary statistics that inform you about the data. They fall into one of four broad categories.[8]

- Measures of frequency, such as counts or percentage, show how frequently something occurs
- Measures of central tendency (a typical value); examples include the mean, median or mode
- Measures of variation such as the standard deviation or range of values
- Measures of position such as deciles or quartiles.

Take time to review the output, as it will give you insight into your data and may provide some surprising results.

It's also important to understand how many records are in each class; for example, a field in a credit card portfolio could denote classic, gold or platinum cards. Is the portfolio split in a way that matches expectations?

Before you look at your results, think about what you expect to see, then compare your expectation with the results. Do the results match your expectation? If not, why not? Is the data telling you something surprising and unexpected?

Now that we have a good idea of the individual fields and how they are distributed, it is time to look at correlations.

Correlations

Correlation does not imply causation. You cannot deduce a cause-and-effect relationship between two variables simply because they are correlated.[9]

Correlation does not imply causation.

For a bit of fun, check out this article on bizarre correlations. https://www.buzzfeednews.com/article/kjh2110/the-10-most-bizarre-correlations

Pearson's correlation coefficient is one of the most commonly used methods to calculate correlations. A correlation of 1 = a perfect positive correlation. A correlation of -1 = a perfect negative correlation (one goes up, the other goes down). And a correlation of 0 = no correlation at all.

Understanding which variables are correlated is essential, as is recognising whether there is a lagged correlated effect. For example, if we see an increase in early-stage arrears, there will probably be an increase in late-stage arrears and a subsequent increase in gross charge-off.

It's useful to know this and receive feedback from the collections team about (for example) incorrectly captured debt orders. That way, we can review the debt orders, identify any that were incorrectly captured and rectify the issue before late-stage arrears and subsequent gross charge-off are materially impacted.

003: Data validations

Having run through EDA, you may be wondering about data validations – haven't we just done that?

Well, no. During EDA, you get a good sense of the data. If you've done a great job of EDA, you'll have developed intuition about the data and understand how the variables interact. Don't panic if you don't yet feel this way; it comes with experience and lots of data exploratory work.

By data validations, I mean double-checking the data against the host system. If your data comes from a data warehouse, you will expect it to match, as, usually, work has been done to ensure that the data going into the DWH is accurate.

However, if you're looking at data extracted and stored in a data lake with no validations performed, you should definitely confirm what you are looking at.

You might wonder why not do this *before* EDA? I suppose you could, but my preference is to ensure I have a reasonable understanding of the data, then chat with the ops people so I can understand the data from their point of view. They are our friends and have insight into the data we likely won't have.

While front-line ops people might not be able to do your job, I'm prepared to bet a coffee that most analysts would not survive a day in ops. Use the opportunity to learn about their processes and how they use the system. Learn their pain points and what they understand about the data they use and capture. This will give you greater insight into what you see in the data and help you develop relationships outside your team.

> **Most analysts would not survive a day in ops.**

When you spend time with your favourite ops people, double-check that the data you're seeing is what is on the system. I mean this quite literally. Use a reference number such as an application or account number. Check that the field contents in your dataset match those on the host system. If they don't, find out what you're looking at. If they do match, confirm that you understand how the data came to be.

004: Additional considerations

Ethics

Although I could write volumes on ethics, especially as they relate to financial services and analysis, I'll keep it short and sweet.

Let's start with a fairly simple definition: Data ethics is concerned with how data is collected, generated, analysed and used.[10] Essentially, it is concerned with the practices people and organisations employ when making use of data. It's worth noting that a key objective of data ethics is ensuring that people and society are not adversely impacted by how data is used.[11]

The purpose of analytics is to use data to drive change. Maintaining robust ethical standards means we can drive meaningful change that benefits people and society.

There are benefits to using data ethically. One of the most important is ensuring that customers and applicants are treated fairly and not discriminated against. Strong ethical standards mean you and your organisation can demonstrate that decision-making is free of bias. This builds loyalty and trust with your customer base, enhancing reputation and brand value.[12]

> The purpose of analytics is to use data to drive change.

Another benefit is complying with data privacy legislation and regulations. Being on the right side of the regulator is generally considered a very good idea.

De-identify data that will be analysed. You can always create a unique matchkey to re-identify it later if that is necessary for operational purposes.

Data sources

Where do you source your data? If it is from a DWH, then lucky you. A different group of people is likely responsible for ensuring that it is clean and properly transformed, etc. There's usually a good data dictionary to go along with it, and a star schema or documentation that tells you how the tables join, the fields, data types, etc.

However, if you're pulling data from the web or a data lake, you may not be quite so fortunate. You will need to consider the stability of the information. How frequently are datasets added to the data lake? Are there gaps or overlaps in the data that you're extracting? How will you find out if there are any changes?

There is an extraordinary amount of data available, so we need to understand how it gets to the point where we can extract it for analysis. To use data analysis in the real world, we need to be able to operationalise it — often in real-time. That means we must understand how the field(s) we want to use are made available from an operational point of view.

Once we know and understand this, we're in a position to use the data, knowing that we have a thorough understanding of the impact of using a particular data source. It also means that if things go pear-shaped, we ought to be able to troubleshoot reasonably rapidly.

Module 0: Points to ponder

Having worked through this module, you'll now understand what it means to import and prep data before you're ready to tackle your analysis. Here are some key questions to consider:

- Can I source all my data reliably and ethically (meaning: am I using the data in a manner consistent with the consented permissions)?
- Do I understand my data well, how it is distributed, what each field means, the data types, etc.?
- Do I understand how my data elements are related to one another?
- Do I understand where my data comes from, whether it is static or updated? And if it is updated, how frequently?
- Do I understand whether I have any missing values and what that means?

This part of analytics may not be the most interesting — some analysts consider it downright dull. However, doing this piece well will save you pain and stress in the long term, as you will be able to identify and exclude variables that are either too closely correlated or have too many missing values to be reliable.

As an analyst, the last thing you want to do is raise a red flag, or highlight a potential game changer, only to discover that the data you're using hasn't been reliably captured.

Module 1

Credit Risk Analytics Fundamentals

This module focuses on the fundamentals of credit risk. This stuff is specific to credit risk, and if you don't understand it, you will struggle to understand why you're seeing what you're seeing in your portfolio, reports and analysis.

We'll look primarily at definitions and concepts. What they are, why they're important, how we use them, and the impact you can have once you have a grasp on them.

Before we dive into details, let's take a quick look at two terms that confused me when I started as a junior credit risk analyst.

The credit risk life cycle and the credit cycle.

Initially, I thought people were using these terms interchangeably. Remember, I came from a science background – no economics or business courses, all sciences and a smattering of arts.

Then I discovered the difference between the two cycles.

The credit risk life cycle

This term refers to the cycle that accounts progress through, starting with applications entering account originations.

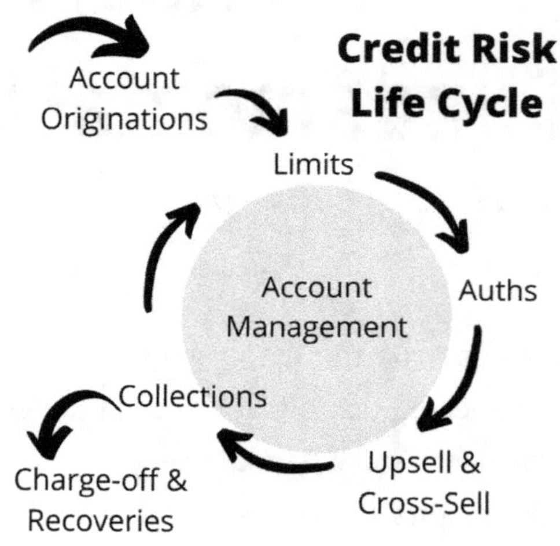

Figure 1 The credit risk life cycle

If an application is approved, it becomes an account, and so begins account management. It's an umbrella term that describes all the areas and decisions an account may go through. These include: limit management, where limits are increased or decreased, auths (authorisations) where individual transactions are assessed for approval; marketing activities such as upsell or cross-sell and collections, where, should an account fail to meet its payment obligations, it will be treated. From collections, an account may continue to fail to meet its payment obligations and eventually be charged-off, or it may rehabilitate and continue within the credit risk life cycle.

The credit cycle

The credit cycle is something else entirely; it describes interest rates and the ease of access to credit. Economists tend to talk about credit cycles and where we are in them. For example, the contracting phase of a credit cycle would see a tendency toward more conservative credit policies, such as an increase in scorecard cut-off scores and a greater strictness applied to policy and business rules. In general, it becomes more difficult to access credit.[13]

When the credit cycle is in an expansion phase, we see interest rates reducing, easy access to credit, and, generally, a more permissive approach to granting credit.[14]

The credit risk life cycle exists during both periods of expansion and contraction; strategies and business rules are modified in line with the phase of the credit cycle in which financial services institutions find themselves.

101: Policy rules vs business rules

Many people think of policy rules and business rules as the same thing. I prefer to break them out.

Policy rules are unlikely to change. They ensure that your decisions comply with legal and regulatory frameworks. For example, in the geographies I have worked in, a minor (someone under the age of 18) cannot enter into a credit contract. If a lender enters into a contract with a minor, that contract cannot be enforced. Therefore, all lenders have a policy rule in place that stipulates that any applicant under the age of 18 is an automatic decline. There is no need to review the application. It doesn't matter what other information is provided, as the age of the applicant means that the application must be declined because, legally, the credit contract cannot be enforced.

Some lenders are not keen to lend to individuals younger than 21 years of age, perhaps thinking that these individuals are also too high risk. Even then a credit manager may decide to approve such an individual under exceptional circumstances. Under these circumstances, I would typically suggest implementing a business rule where all applicants under the age of 21 are automatically declined.

At this point, you may be wondering about the real difference between these two rules. Afterall, in both cases, all applicants are automatically declined. The key difference is this:

- Under the policy rule (age < 18), the decline may not be overridden by anyone.
- Under the business rule (age < 21), the decline may be overridden in exceptional circumstances by a person with the appropriate authority.

The order in which these rules are applied is important. I always recommend implementing policy rules first. From a practical point of view, it makes little difference as an application triggering a policy rule will always be declined.

From a logical point of view, it makes sense to implement the rules so that once an application has triggered a policy rule, all further processing stops and the application is declined. This reduces the demand on system resources as once a policy rule has been triggered, no other information will change the decision.

Business rules can be set to decline applications or refer them for underwriting.

It may also make sense to implement rules so that the policy rules most likely to be triggered are applied first, followed by the decline rules less likely to be triggered. Again, this minimises processing time for applications that trigger a decline policy rule.

When it comes to business rules, I recommend a different approach. Business rules can be set to decline applications or refer them for underwriting. All business rules should be applied, regardless of the outcome. Once an application has passed through all the rules, it should continue through the application process. Any decision to decline, refer or approve the application is made at the end of the process.

Why? If a declined applicant requests a review of the decision, the underwriting team have all the information at their fingertips. They can manually review the decision without having to process the application again.

The second reason I like having all the information available is for reporting and analysis. We will cover this in more detail later, but keep in mind that we need the data before doing any analysis.

102: Good/bad definition

Goods and bads! This term can be quite triggering if you've never come across it before. Credit risk analysts use goods and bads as a kind of shorthand — and they're not describing the customer or account holder. We use the terms good and bad to describe the performance on the account.

> Credit risk analysts use goods and bads as a kind of shorthand.

Saying an account is good means we're really happy with its performance. And in a perfect world, we would only accept applications that meet our definition of good.[15]

On the other hand, when we talk about bad accounts, we are describing the account performance, not passing judgement on the account holder or customer. We describe account performance as bad when, in a perfect world, we would have been able to accurately predict that the performance on the account would not have met our expectations and we would have declined them.

There is a third group called indeterminates. Essentially this means that, based on account performance, we cannot determine whether performance is good or bad. We are undecided on this group of applications. Although they are not the subject of this book, scorecard developers are very interested in the indeterminate group. They apply principles to ensure that the group is not too big or too small.

So, as a rule of thumb, there are generally two good/bad definitions, and a company would typically only choose one. Let's look at the differences.

Good/bad definition #1

Good accounts are typically where the worst delinquency in the past 12-24 months is up to date (UTD), or one or two cycles in arrears. In bad accounts, the worst delinquency is four or more cycles in arrears (this includes accounts that are charged-off or written-off). Accounts that reach a maximum of three cycles in arrears over the 12-24 months are known as indeterminates, neither good nor bad.

Good/bad definition #2

Good accounts are typically where the worst delinquency on the account in the past 12-24 months is up to date (UTD) or one cycle in arrears. Bad accounts are where the worst delinquency on the account is three or more cycles in arrears (this includes accounts that are charged-off or written-off). Accounts that reach a maximum of two cycles in arrears over 12-24 months are known as indeterminates, neither good nor bad.

Your scorecard development team will recommend the best good/bad definition to use. The key consideration is the volumes of accounts classified as indeterminate and bad. I would expect more good accounts than bad or indeterminate ones. If not, I would be concerned about the profitability of the credit portfolio.

Determining the optimal good/bad definition is a tradeoff between the majority of accounts that will reach the bad definition having enough time to do so, and ensuring sufficient volumes for robust analytics.

> **Look at the ratio of goods to bads.**

In essence, the performance window needs to be as short as possible (to ensure that we're using the freshest data) and as long as necessary (to ensure that account performance has enough time to mature).

Odds

The good/bad odds (GBOdds) look at the ratio of goods to bads.

$$GBOdds = \frac{Goods}{Bads}$$

They are typically recorded to 2 decimal places. The higher the odds, the better the performance of that group of accounts.

Bad rate

Bad rate also considers the relationship between good and bad accounts. In this case, bads are expressed as a percentage of all accounts:

$$Bad\ Rate = \left(\frac{Bads}{All\ Accounts} \right) \%$$

Bad rate is also typically recorded to two decimal places. Although in this case, the higher the percentage, the worse the performance of that group of accounts.

103: Using scorecards

Scorecards are one of our most essential tools for assessing risk. Typically, lower scores indicate higher risk, and higher scores indicate lower risk. There are a plethora of books that cover scorecards and scoring in detail, so, I won't do that here.

Scorecards are designed to rank order applications or accounts. Those scores are then used in credit risk strategies to help define what action to apply to an application or account.

There are several types of scorecards. They're built using different information and are used at various points of the credit risk life cycle.

There are several key reasons to use scorecards and when used appropriately, risk scores can effectively reduce risk:

- They decrease bad debt by reducing exposure on high-risk accounts.
- Scorecards can increase automation rates and time-to-decision by automatically handling obvious decisions.
- They increase consistency by ensuring that applicants and account holders are treated equally, objectively and fairly across the organisation and decision points.
- Scorecards can help increase revenues and sales by improving approval rates (whilst maintaining bad debt rates) and ensuring that credit-worthy account holders are included in credit limit increase campaigns.[16]

Application scores

Application scores are typically built using demographic information, such as age, region, marital status and number of dependents. This information is considered static as it doesn't change or only does so slowly. It's also worth noting that an application usually only happens once and is assessed at that point. Any subsequent application is assessed independently of the earlier application. Applications are normally scored using an application scorecard.

Behaviour scores

Behaviour scores are generally recalculated each month based on account performance using a behaviour scorecard. These scores are used within account management strategies, such as limit management, delinquency or arrears management, overlimit management and auths management to determine appropriate actions.

Behaviour scores may also be used in cross-sell campaigns or when assessing the application risk of a known customer for a subsequent product. These scores often have segments based on the state of the account at the point of scoring. However, the scores are calculated so analysts can use them without having detailed knowledge of the underlying segmentation.

Bureau scores

These scores are created by credit bureaux and contain information held on individuals sourced from a wide range of industries and organisations. Bureau scores are usually built at a customer level, and summarise an individual's performance across all their accounts.

Credit bureau scores can be used effectively at all stages of the credit risk life cycle and are used at the point of origination to better segment application risk. They are also often used within credit limit management, arrears management and cross-sell strategies and initiatives.

Credit bureau scores add depth to what we already know about our applicants and customers.

Propensity scores

We use propensity scores when determining an either/or situation. Will this individual respond to the offer (Y/N)? Will they use this credit facility if it is extended to them?[17]

Payment projection scores

A payment projection score is used for late-stage delinquent accounts. These include accounts that are flagged as 'judgement'. When a judgement has been made against the account, it is listed with the credit bureaux. Accounts are considered late stage once they have reached the bad definition used for the behaviour score, typically three or four cycles delinquent but not yet charged-off.

Recovery scores

This is used on accounts that have already been charged-off. Recovery scores determine what proportion of the outstanding balance will likely be repaid over a defined period. These scores prioritise post charge-off activity on accounts, including debt sales where they may influence the price likely to be achieved.

Continuous scores

A continuous score predicts the likelihood of a continuous outcome. Payment projection scores and recovery scores are examples of these. The question is usually, 'What proportion of the balance outstanding on this account is likely to be repaid?'

Binary scores

Binary scores forecast the likelihood of an event happening. For example, is this account likely to reach the bad definition if we decide to extend credit?

104: Interpreting scores

When a scorecard developer creates your scorecard, they will ensure you can interpret it (or they certainly should!). Why? So you have a starting point when looking at the applications or accounts with an expected risk and can treat them accordingly.[18]

> The credit risk analyst needs to know two key pieces of information.

As a credit risk analyst, you don't need to know how to set the points on the scorecard to ensure that the definition is met, but it is helpful to understand the process.

Just as scorecards can have different performance definitions, they can also have different meanings. The credit risk analyst needs to know two key pieces of information. The first is the standard score to odds relationship and the second is the points to double the odds.

Standard score to odds relationship

The standard score to odds relationship is usually in the middle of the scorecard range. Scorecards typically range from 0 to 1000, with lower scores indicating higher risk accounts and higher scores indicating better risk accounts. There are often exclusion scores, which are reasons why an application or account has not been scored. They are usually given extremely low numeric values, so when it comes to reporting, you can easily see how many records were not scored and why.

Scorecard developers can choose any scaling that works for them. My preference is for a standard, as this makes it easier to remember what it is. Most behaviour scores I have worked with have a standard score to odds relationship as follows:

Score of 660 = GBOdds of 15:1

That means all accounts that score 660 points on the behaviour scorecard have expected GBOdds of 15 goods for every one bad account.

Score (or points) to double the odds

The second important score metric you need to know is the score or number of points required to double (or halve) the odds. In most behaviour scores I've worked with, the points to double the odds (PDO) are 15. In other words, an account with a score of 675 (660+15) has GBOdds of 30:1. That means in a group of accounts with a behaviour score of 675, 30 will likely have good performance for every one with bad performance.

Similarly, a group of accounts that scores 615 (660-15) has GBOdds of 7.5:1. This means 15 are likely to have good performance for every two accounts with bad performance.

Understanding the standard score to odds relationship and the PDO of a scorecard means you can use it within strategies to apply actions to groups of accounts or applications that are likely to perform similarly.

Scorecard developers often use different standard score to odds and PDO relationships for different types of scorecards. They do so to make analysts' lives easier.

105: Tilt by risk

Tilt by risk means we take a more conservative approach on high risk applications and accounts, and a more permissive or lenient approach on low risk applications or accounts.

In practical terms, that means more actions are applied to higher risk applications or accounts to mitigate the risk of the application or account reaching the bad definition. Conversely, fewer (or zero) actions are applied to lower risk applications or accounts.

Credit risk analysts do this to maintain operational efficiency and ensure we don't need to increase staffing costs significantly. It makes sense that increasing the amount of activity, verification and underwriting on one group of applications, reduces the amount of activity, verification and underwriting required on a different (better risk) group.

Tilt by risk means we take a more conservative approach on high risk applications and accounts, and a more permissive or lenient approach on low risk applications or accounts.

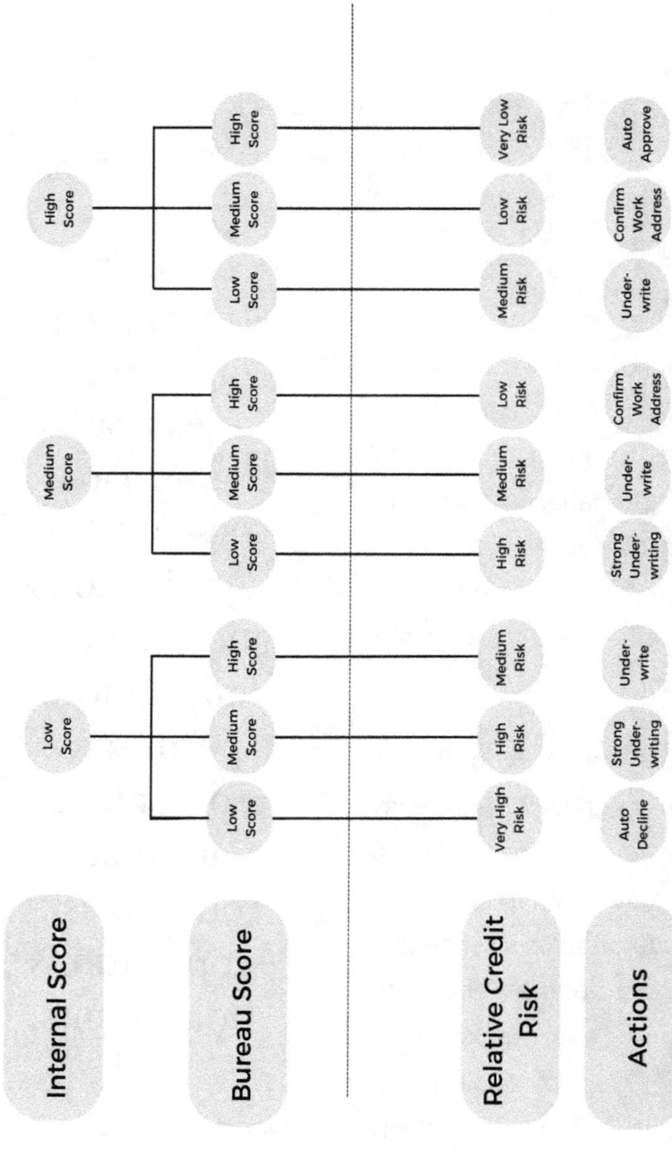

Figure 2 Tilt by risk, where higher risk applications have more actions applied than lower risk applications

106: Clean testing

No, clean testing doesn't involve soap or a shower. It simply means multiple tests are conducted without interfering with each another. We're trying to establish whether the actions we apply to the challenger group of accounts or applications deliver better results than the champion strategy actions.

To measure the results of the test and determine whether the test was successful, we need to ensure that two conditions are met:

Firstly, the applications or accounts in each group (champions and challengers) should be statistically similar. That means looking at various measures (particularly ones we may be interested in measuring later) that show no statistical differences between the groups. For example, any statistical differences between groups (income, application score, bureau score, etc.) are insignificant. This is important because if we see differences in accept rates, credit limits, balance build, interest revenues or delinquency when measuring the results at the end of the test, we want to know that these differences occurred during testing.

The second condition is that we don't mix and match tests. Applications and accounts impacted by one test or challenger strategy should not be affected by another. The reason? If a group of accounts is impacted by more than one test, you can't know which test is responsible. This matters because tests often involve increased manual intervention for a group of accounts, which is offset by a decrease in manual intervention for other applications or accounts. And it is important to understand which actions were responsible for the result.

Testing and data are not trucks: you cannot just back out differences that were built in at the start or confounding factors that crept into the test because of poor planning and execution.

107: Decline overrides

Banks and financial services organisations typically auto-decline a proportion of applications deemed too high risk. These are not the policy declines, such as <18 years, as we discussed earlier. Instead, these applications pass the policy rules but have other factors that deem them too high risk to consider accepting. Therefore, they are automatically declined by the system, with no human intervention. These applications may have triggered decline business rules, or several refer business rules, or perhaps their application bureau score is too low. Typically these accounts are considered such high risk that they are not underwritten, as the overall decline rate for this group of applications means resources could be better deployed in underwriting other applications.

Occasionally one of these applicants may call the organisation and ask for their application for credit to be reassessed.

Remember, the risk associated with an application is the risk, or likelihood, that the accepted application will reach the bad definition within a defined time period. There's no guarantee that the accepted application will reach the bad definition. That means even if the odds are 1:1000 (one good for every 1000 bad accounts), there is still one good account.

When an automatically declined account is subsequently approved, it is known as a decline override. It is essential to track how many of these happen each month. If there are too many, and the subsequent performance on those accounts is acceptable, it may indicate that the strategy settings ought to be reviewed. If there are too many and subsequent performance is not acceptable, we need to engage with the operations team to understand why they're overriding these applications and share the subsequent performance. Ultimately, poor performance on decline overrides increases costs, not only in terms of originations operational efficiency. Arrears management operational costs, collective provisions costs and gross charge-off costs all increase.

$$\textit{Decline Override Rate} = \frac{\textit{Number of decline overrides}}{\textit{Number of automated declines (initial decision)}}\%$$

If your decline override rate exceeds 5%, look closer to understand performance and determine what actions are necessary.

108: Auto-decisioning

One of the key objectives when designing credit risk strategies is to increase automation rates; to boost the number of applications that are appropriately approved or declined without human intervention. To do this, we track the automation rate, typically on a weekly and monthly basis.

Auto-decisioned applications are the sum of applications that were either approved or declined on the initial decision.

$$Automation\ Rate = \frac{Number\ of\ auto\text{-}decisioned\ applications}{Number\ of\ applications\ received}\ \%$$

An increase in the automation rate means that the organisation can process more applications without a corresponding increase in underwriting staff. Conversely, a decrease in the automation rate means that you may require more staff to maintain application assessment and the time taken to assess those applications. These are important considerations for the operations teams. By determining whether a change in strategy will materially change the automation rate, you can front-foot conversations with the operations teams and ensure that all parties understand the implications of the strategy change.

109: Recency vs delinquency vs days past due

Recency, delinquency and days past due (DPD) are measures used to assess less-than-ideal payment behaviour.

Recency refers to the time between the present day and when the customer last made a qualifying payment. It is measured in days which are sometimes lumped into 30-day buckets to approximate months.

Days past due is a count of the number of days that an account has not been up to date. It is typically applied to loans and, unsurprisingly, it is measured in days. As with recency, the days are sometimes lumped into 30-day buckets to approximate months.

Delinquency (Delq) counts how many qualifying payments the customer has failed to make.

A qualifying payment is usually set in the host system. Essentially, it is a 'fudge' factor that allows the system to say, 'Yes, this customer has made a payment', even if it is less than the amount due on the statement.

Let me illustrate this by way of example:

On the account statement, the minimum amount due is $97.15. If the customer pays $97.00, would that be enough to constitute a payment? What about $95.00 or $90.00?

Qualifying payments are typically set at about 95% of the minimum amount due so that a customer doesn't go into arrears for a small amount unpaid.

110: Adverse selection

If you spend enough time with credit risk people, you'll hear about adverse selection. Adverse selection means your organisation may inadvertently take on more risk than expected.

> Adverse selection means your organisation may inadvertently take on more risk than expected.

Wikipedia defines adverse selection as 'a market situation where buyers and sellers have different information'.[19]

From a retail consumer credit risk point of view, adverse selection happens when an organisation makes an offer to individuals with a wide variety of credit risks. Low-risk people can get credit at good rates from a range of credit providers, whereas high-risk individuals cannot and may choose to accept whatever credit is on offer.

If banks or financial service providers offer credit with terms less favourable than their competitors, they may find lower-risk individuals do not take up the offer because they can get better terms elsewhere. The company then finds that delinquency and bad rates are higher than anticipated for this particular tranche of business.

Adverse selection comes into play in several ways. It generally means that the seller (the financial services organisation offering credit) doesn't have all the information available. The organisation may think it is accepting a marginal risk of X%, however the risk could be materially higher.

Keep this in mind when developing new-to-market offers. Assuming that the best risk people will take up your offer may be inaccurate if those individuals have access to better offers.

Module 1: Points to ponder

This module has covered many essential credit risk concepts. We looked at policy and business rules and the different purposes they serve. We considered definitions that might apply when we define account performance as good or bad. There was plenty of talk about scorecards, how to interpret scores, and why that is important and necessary. We also discussed some key concepts credit risk analysts use and consider when analysing data.

Here are a few key questions to keep in mind:

- Am I treating applications or accounts that represent similar risks to the business consistently?
- Have I ensured that all tests I run are free from unexplained interference? If not, what is my plan? (Remember, analysis isn't a truck; you cannot just reverse any initial bias introduced through ill-considered methodology.)
- Do I have a solid understanding of when changes that may influence results were implemented? Create a chronology log to record major strategy and policy rule changes, so everyone knows what happened and when.

Module 2

Credit Risk Essentials

Now that you understand the terminology and key concepts, it is time to dive into more exciting stuff.

The concepts discussed here are fundamental to many pieces of credit risk analytics. I'm a fan of using first principles whenever I tackle or start to unpack an issue. Using the information covered in Module 0 and Module 1, with what we're about to discuss here, you will be well-placed to tackle any number of credit risk challenges.

201: Observation and performance windows

Whether we want to evaluate if a strategy is working, confirm a business rule is delivering as expected, or understand what's been happening so we can propose a better solution, we need to look at some observations. And then we need to understand what happened.

We do this by building and using observation and performance windows.

The observation window

This is *when* stuff happened — **before,** or at the point of, the decision.

There are several considerations here:

1. We cannot include any performance variables – things that happened *after* the decision.
2. We must consider seasonality. That refers to how delinquency rates change depending on the time of year. Typically, they reduce in the lead-up to Christmas and then increase. When doing analytics on applications, I use 12 months to cover seasonality.

3. We need to know whether there were changes to the process we're about to analyse. For example, the analysis may yield unexpected results if the scorecards were replaced part way through the observation window.

The performance window

This is as important as the observation window. How long should your performance window be? The answer is not quite as long as a piece of string, and there are some guidelines and rules of thumb that you can apply.

If you have a scorecard, I recommend using the performance window definition. Scorecard developers will have worked out how long the window ought to be to ensure that accounts that are likely to reach the bad definition have done so.

The performance window for each record starts when the decision being analysed is made. So, the performance window for applications starts with the accept date.

Of course, there are caveats and considerations. Sometimes analysts want to do some quick and dirty or cheap and cheerful analytics to get an idea of whether things are going in the right direction. This niggling concern or intuition often comes with years of experience.

We can, if necessary, use a short performance window (3-6 rather than 12-24 months) by using an early estimator or proxy of the bad definition. If I were concerned and needed an early look at whether something was weird, I would probably look at a 3-6 month performance window (and a similarly truncated observation window) **knowing** the weaknesses and use one payment missed as a proxy for the bad definition.

When doing this, we must be somewhat cautious about drawing conclusions!

Those considerations aside, I would generally regard a 12-month observation window and a 12-month performance window as sufficient.

202: 'Breaking' scorecards

I once really upset a CEO by stating that the purpose of a credit risk strategy is to break the scorecard. He was not happy....

I should probably explain what I meant.

When scorecards are built, the scores have meaning; higher scores typically indicate lower risk, and lower scores indicate higher risk. Scorecards have a standard score to odds relationship and specific points to double the odds. We might build an application scorecard so that a score of 200 gives good/bad odds of 20:1, and 20 points double the odds.

That would mean a score of 220 would give good/bad odds of 40:1, and a score of 180 would give good/bad odds of 10:1.

We don't truly break scorecards when we design strategies, but by appropriately applying tilt-by-risk to our strategies, the observed odds for higher scoring records underperform compared to the expected odds. And the observed odds for the lower scoring records outperform when compared to the expected odds. This is illustrated in figure 3.

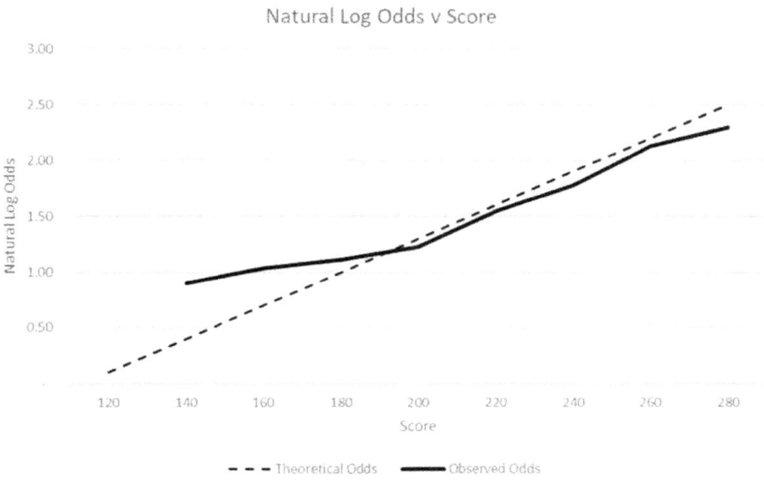

Figure 3 Breaking the scorecard

The natural log odds is shown on the vertical axis and the score is on the horizontal axis. We use the natural log odds because it translates the expected performance into a straight line – remember that every 20 points double the odds. The dashed line represents the expected odds, with the expected odds increasing as the score increases.

The solid line shows the observed odds. That is what I mean when I say we broke the scorecard. We would not accept all applications at low score where the expected performance is poor. Instead, we would underwrite these applications. The acceptance rate in these lower scores bands is expected to be low. Because our underwriters have cherry-picked the best of the bunch, we see that the observed performance is materially better than expected.

Conversely, we would not underwrite applications at the high end of the scored population. We would auto-approve applications that met our regulatory obligations (such as responsible lending) and policy rules. This may result in performance being slightly lower than the expected performance.

203: Transition matrices

Transition matrices may be ugly beasts. They will certainly mangle your brain the first time you come across one, but they are incredibly useful. They tell

> Transition matrices may be ugly beasts.

you how accounts move from their state of arrears or delinquency last month to their state of arrears or delinquency this month. A transition matrix typically shows the percentage balance by row. The number of accounts, average balance, balances or percentage balances can also be used. The important thing to remember here is that the metric (number of accounts, average balance, balances etc.) used is always summed by row.

Transition Matrix		Delinquency this month							
		UTD	Delq1	Delq2	Delq3	Delq4	Delq5	Delq6	GCO
Delinquency last month	UTD	😃😃😃	🙁						🙁
	Delq1	😃😃😃	😐	🙁					🙁
	Delq2	😃😃😃	🙂	😐	🙁				🙁
	Delq3	😃😃😃	🙂	🙂	😐	🙁			🙁
	Delq4	😃😃😃	🙂	🙂	🙂	😐	🙁		🙁
	Delq5	😃😃😃	🙂	🙂	🙂	🙂	😐	🙁	🙁
	Delq6	😃😃😃	🙂	🙂	🙂	🙂	🙂	😐	🙁

Figure 4 Example transition matrix

This is what you would expect to see in a transition matrix, so let's step through it slowly.

The rows show the level of delinquency associated with accounts last month and the columns show the level of delinquency associated with accounts this month.

Forward roll rates

The sad face ☹ cells show accounts where no qualifying payment was made. The delinquency on those accounts is higher this month than last. It is known as the roll rate, as accounts have rolled into a higher level of delinquency.

In some cases, accounts may have been charged-off. Accounts in lower levels of delinquency are typically charged-off at lower rates than accounts in higher levels.

Mill rates

☺ The ambivalent face cells show accounts where a single qualifying payment was made, known as the mill rate. The payment on these accounts was sufficient to prevent the account from becoming more delinquent, but insufficient to make them less delinquent.

Partial cure rates

The single smiley face cells show the partial cure rate. This happens when the payment on an account is more than a single qualifying payment, but not enough to bring the account back into order.

Cure rates

And finally, the triple smiley face cells show the cure rate. The payment made on these accounts is sufficient to cover all the arrears and bring the account up to date.

The roll rates at earlier delinquency levels are lower than the corresponding roll rates of more delinquent accounts. Conversely, the cure rates are higher.

Building transition matrices

To build a transition matrix, we need the following information for all accounts on book that were not charged off at last month's statement date:

- Account number
- Delinquency last month
- Balance as at statement date last month
- Delinquency this month
- Charge-off status this month.

Make sure you have one record per account, with these fields clearly identified. This usually requires sorting and merging data by account number. I create a single field that combines this month's delinquency and gross charge-off into a single field (simply because it makes the creation of the pivot or cross tab more straightforward). Create a pivot table or cross matrix showing last month's delinquency on the left-hand side and this month's delinquency and charge-off across the top of the matrix table. Populate the cells with last month's balance or number of accounts. Note that the balance for charged-off accounts will be the amount charged-off, unless it is captured in last month's balance at statement date.

Sum the totals for each row.

Calculate the rates as the percentage of balance (or count) in each cell, divided by the row total.

Interpreting transition matrices

Transition matrices help us understand why we may see increases in the delinquency profile. If we know we have implemented a drive to reduce late-stage arrears (delinquency 4 or more), we may see an unexpected increase in delinquency 3 in the monthly reporting. Reviewing the transition matrix allows us to determine whether the increase in balances in delinquency 3 was because more accounts rolled into delq3 from delq2, which would be bad. Or perhaps the increase in delq3 resulted from the drive to reduce late-stage arrears, which would be good and in line with what was intended.

Transition matrices are another great way to compare strategy performance and see whether the strategy is delivering as expected. Once we have the transition matrices, we can use them to estimate likely future gross charge-off (more on that in Module 3).

These reports contain plenty of information, although they are not necessarily the most intuitive. However, they are fantastic tools — especially when the delinquency profile doesn't look quite right. We need to decide whether to be concerned and, if so, what our next course of action should be.

204: Calculating theoretical breakeven odds

The breakeven odds of a portfolio is a theoretical number. It is a useful guide to setting initial cut-off scores if we have nothing else to work with. Essentially, we're trying to estimate how many good accounts are required to offset one bad account.

> The breakeven odds of a portfolio is a theoretical number.

Several things need to be taken into consideration:

- Average credit limit on new accounts
- Average good and bad balances
- Annual interest rate.

I usually use a 12-month ballpark – after all, this theoretical number is intended as a guideline, a starting point for further conversation.

Key considerations

We start by considering the average credit limit assigned to new accounts because that is the average maximum possible balance. We then look at average good and bad balances (again, over 12 months). When considering them, we often observe that the bad balances are higher than the good balances, which may be a cause for concern.

At this point, you may be wondering why bad balances would be higher than good balances?

People with good credit scores tend to spend within their means, whereas those with lower credit scores appear more optimistic about how much they can actually repay. Individuals with higher scores also often transact on their card products – meaning they pay their balance in full each month. Lower scoring individuals tend to pay the minimum required, so their balance increases month-on-month.

These days, with increased scrutiny on responsible lending legislation, I would expect to see a smaller gap between good and bad balances. If you're operating in an environment where responsible lending isn't applied strongly (or strongly enough) you may find that the average bad balances are materially higher than the average good balances. If this is the case, you may want to revisit your credit limit setting strategy.

Once we have an average good balance, average bad balance and annual interest rate, we can calculate the estimated break-even odds.

For good accounts, the estimated profit is the annual interest rate applied to the average good balance outstanding. We expect to be paid, and therefore to earn interest.

Have you spotted the flaw in this back-of-the-envelope calculation?

In revolving credit portfolios, good accounts typically transact or revolve at a lower rate, so we're unlikely to earn all the interest in the calculation above. We estimate we will charge off the average outstanding balance for bad accounts. Again, this argument is flawed because we know we will not charge off all these accounts.

> This calculation is a useful starting point.

Nonetheless, this calculation is a useful starting point for ballparking your cut-off and deciding how much risk you want to take.

Example

Average good balance: $2500

Average bad balance: $2750

Annual interest rate: 15%

Estimated interest earned (profit) on good balance: $375 ($2500*15%)

Therefore, in this example, we would need eight good accounts to offset one bad account (8*$375 = $3000, whilst 7*$375 = $2625). At the margin, we're earning $3000 (on the eight good accounts) and losing $2750 for each bad account, leaving $250 in profit.

Note that if the interest rate was 25%, we would need five good accounts to offset one bad account. Remember, these really are rough calculations and do not factor in all costs and revenues. We're trying to determine whether we can bring in an additional tranche of business once all the costs are accounted for. In doing so, we must be sure that it is wholly profitable.

This process is useful for scorecard cut-off setting and ensuring that your initial limits are a good fit (good and bad balances aren't too far apart). That means your risk team and other stakeholders can have an informed conversation about what level of risk they want to take on board. It also means that you can have a conversation about a loss-leading offer. That's if you can demonstrate that over time the value of the good accounts compensates for balances that are charged off.

205: Comprehensive credit bureau information

In New Zealand, we have three credit bureaux. Equifax, Centrix and illion.

Individuals can get a free copy of their credit report from each bureau. A credit score is typically a three-digit number, between 1 and 1000. This number represents a summary of your behaviour concerning your credit obligations. It summarises information, such as recent applications for credit, any defaults, the credit limit on facilities, and your repayment history over the previous 24 months.[20]

Comprehensive credit reporting (CCR) became permissible in New Zealand in 2012. With the introduction of CCR, credit reporters can collect additional information (provided all consents have been obtained). Previously, credit providers could only report on negative and enquiry information. Under CCR, they can report on the amount of credit extended, the details of the credit provider, the type of credit extended and the most recent 24 months of repayment history.[21]

Notably, lenders may not report the balance on the credit account, only the credit extended.

Factors influencing bureau scores

In other geographies, the amount owed (balance outstanding) can be, and is, reported. Once you know the balance outstanding and credit limit, you can calculate utilisation, which is a handy predictor of credit risk.

Five key categories influence a person's credit score.[22]

- Payment history (~35%)
- Amount owed (~30%) (not available through NZ credit bureaux)
- Length of credit history (~15%)
- New credit (~10%)
- Credit mix (~10%).

In New Zealand, only credit providers who share CCR information may access it. This is outlined in the CCR heads of agreement.[23]

I strongly encourage any organisation to subscribe to CCR, as this means your organisation will have access to repayment history, new credit and the credit mix. All these factors increase your ability to predict risk.

If, as a credit provider, you provide multiple types of credit, you could build a customer score. With all the available information, you could build a score that includes the five categories highlighted above, including utilisation.

206: Strategy Monitoring

So, you've built a new strategy and implemented it – yippee!

Now you need to monitor it. There are several reasons why strategies need to be monitored. Chief amongst them is that we need to know whether it is doing what we expected.

Strategies can be implemented across the full portfolio or a sample, then compared with the champion strategy to determine which wins. They must be monitored, regardless of which approach is adopted.

We monitor them using strategy monitoring reports and compare them through strategy difference reports.

Strategy monitoring reports

These measure key metrics over several months and are dependent on what management area your strategy impacts.

For account origination strategies, I want to measure the metrics that show how my account origination strategy is tracking (e.g., accept rates and limits issued). In account management strategies, I am interested in the metrics associated with the management area I'm trying to affect (e.g., credit limits, balance build and interest earned or delinquencies).

When only one strategy is in place, it is essential to understand what 'good' looks like before you start. That way, you have an idea of what you expect to see, you can compare the actual results with expectations and determine whether your strategy is delivering as expected.

Strategy difference reports

Strategy difference reports are similar to strategy monitoring reports, with one key difference: Two strategies are compared over the same period, using the same key metrics. Any differences in results are attributed to the difference in strategy, meaning a winner can be determined.

Strategies are typically monitored over several months to collect sufficient performance information. This performance information determines whether a strategy wins and ought to be rolled out across the full portfolio.

Module 2: Points to ponder

In this module, we looked at the concepts around observation points and performance periods, and clarified what you need to think about.

Key questions to consider:

- Will all the variables I'm using in my observation window be available before the decision point? This might seem trivial, but if you're using information that is unknown when the decision is made (either to accept the application, or trigger a collections action), it cannot be considered when applications or accounts are routed for decisioning. This could result in some unexpected volumes or actions.
- How will I use this analysis? It's important to think about how you'll use the outcome of your analysis. Are you raising awareness? Might you have to repeat this analysis on a regular or semi-regular basis? Is your ultimate aim to drive change operationally?

Module 3

Advanced Credit Risk Analytics

In this module, we'll cover some of the discrete pieces of analysis that credit risk analysts typically complete. They often rely on concepts that we've discussed in the previous modules.

We bring together all the previously discussed elements, although they may not all be used at the same time. Senior credit risk analysts with broad and deep credit risk technical skills truly shine when they can build and interpret this type of analysis, use their knowledge of the scores the organisation uses and interpret them to best optimise strategies.

301: Vintage analysis

A vintage analysis is a common and popular method of monitoring originations' credit risk. It is sometimes called cohort analysis. The vintage or cohort refers to the origination period under review. Vintages could be months, quarters or years, depending on the purpose of the analysis.

In essence, vintage analysis measures portfolio performance at specific periods after the point of origination. For example, we might look at what proportion of accounts are 30+DPD, or one or more months delinquent, six months after origination. Then we compare credit originating in January with credit originating in March.

> Vintages could be months, quarters or years, depending on the purpose of the analysis.

Although vintage analysis typically measures delinquency and often includes gross charge-off, it could also measure other metrics such as balance build, interest earned, spend, average balance and total payments, etc.

Why vintage analysis is important

Vintage analysis is a powerful tool for measuring or monitoring the risk of a portfolio. Specifically, we can compare risk across cohorts or time periods to determine whether some are unexpectedly riskier than others. Scorecard developers often use vintage analysis to determine a portfolio's performance window (as long as necessary, as short as possible). Vintage analysis can also estimate gross charge-off, particularly in loan portfolios.[24, 25]

To create a vintage analysis report, we need accounts at the point of origination and the associated performance of those accounts.

Building a vintage analysis report

The first step is to decide which portfolio you want to build the report for. For example, if there are several store card portfolios in your stable, creating one for each portfolio would let you compare them. If you only make one report, the analysis may lose subtleties.

If I'm building a vintage report at the same time that I launch a portfolio, then I start collecting data as I build the report. Most of us build these reports on portfolios that have been active for many years. I would want 24-36 months of originations.

There are a couple of reasons for this. We expect to see when the vintage curve flattens, indicating that all the bad accounts have reached the bad definition. And we expect to observe seasonal trends.

Two types of data are required to build a vintage report: originations data and performance data. Let's look at each.

Originations data

We need the account number, the account origination date and the portfolio. This information is summarised into the number of accounts originated by vintage or cohort. Typically, this is by origination month or origination quarter.

To measure something other than the delinquency rate (by count), we need to pull the appropriate denominator metric into the observation data (such as credit limit issued).

Performance data

From a performance data perspective, we gather and measure the relevant fields each month. For example, to determine the 30+ (two cycles delinquent) rate, we need to know each account's delinquency and gross charge-off status each month. Building a spend vintage means knowing the total spend for each account each month, or creating a flag to determine whether there was spend, and using that to determine the proportion of accounts with spend.

There are a plethora of metrics we could create. The key to performance data is gathering this information each month for all accounts that have been originated.

When credit risk analysts talk about vintage analysis, they describe risk measures, usually the 30+ and 90+ (two and four cycles delinquent, respectively) curves. I will focus here on the 30+ rate, as once you understand the principles, you can build any type of vintage analysis.

Building a 30+ DPD or 2+ cycles delinquent vintage analysis

In most organisations, delinquency data and gross charge-off data are stored in separate tables. We include charged-off accounts in reporting because these meet the definition that we're building to. In this case, we're determining the proportion of accounts that are 30+ or 2+ cycles delinquent. If omitted, they will likely be counted in one month (immediately before charge-off occurs) but not in subsequent months. That will mean the vintage curves understate the proportion of accounts that are 30+ DPD/2+ cycles delinquent.

> It is most important to be consistent.

Although there is an argument for using an 'ever' definition, I prefer not to. This definition effectively flags an account as 30+ or 2+ cycles delinquent if it ever reaches that point. It ignores the fact that accounts can rehabilitate. It is the more conservative approach. In my opinion, it is most important to be consistent, so all vintage curves should be calculated the same way for meaningful comparison.

Now that we have the data, let's build the report.

Creating a vintage analysis

In essence, a vintage report shows what proportion of accounts reached the performance definition in the months since they were originated. Summarise the originations data to show the number of new accounts originated for each month.

Vintage Analysis		New Accts	Months since Origination											
			1	2	3	4	5	6	7	8	9	10	11	12
	Sep '21	994												
	Oct '21	982												
	Nov '21	1,019												
	Dec '21	966												
	Jan '22	980												
Origination Month	Feb '22	1,009												
	Mar '22	993												
	Apr '22	952												
	May '22	995												
	Jun '22													
	Jul '22													
	Aug '22													

Count of new accounts originated each month from your observation data.

Figure 5 Shows the beginnings of the vintage analysis

Now let's consider account performance. A vintage report is powerful because it counts the number of months that have occurred since origination. The origination month specifies which tranche we're looking at. All tranches can be compared because we're asking what proportion of accounts opened are 2+ cycles delinquency, five months after they were originated.

The trick is to convert the month into 'months since'. This may sound odd. Let's look at a few examples.

We'll compare three accounts:

Account 1001 was opened on 3 Jan 2021

Account 1002 was opened on 5 Feb 2021

Account 1003 was opened on 8 May 2021

All these accounts were statemented in August 2021.

Account 1001 -> statement date Aug2021 -> cycles delinquent = 2

Account 1002 -> statement date Aug2021 -> cycles delinquent = 4

Account 1003 -> statement date Aug2021 -> cycles delinquent = 1

(It just so happens that all these accounts have missed payments.)

In a vintage analysis, we're interested in the statement date as it is used to calculate the months since the account was opened.

Account 1001 was opened in Jan 2021; therefore, there are seven months of performance on the account at the August statement date.

Account 1002 was opened in Feb 2021; therefore, there are six months of performance on the account at the August statement date.

Account 1003 was opened in May 2021; therefore, there are three months of performance on the account at the August statement date.

Next month, when the September data is available, we will have eight months of performance data for account 1001, seven months for account 1002 and four months for account 1003.

With that principle in mind, we can build the performance aspect of a vintage analysis report.

Vintage Analysis (2+ Cycles Delq)		New Accts	Months since Origination											
			1	2	3	4	5	6	7	8	9	10	11	12
Origination Month	Sep '21	994	0	0	3	4	12	15	23	29	52			
	Oct '21	982	0	0	3	4	12	15	22	30				
	Nov '21	1,019	0	0	2	2	10	13	18					
	Dec '21	966	0	0	3	3	13	15						
	Jan '22	980	0	0	3	4	11							
	Feb '22	1,009	0	0	4	4								
	Mar '22	993	0	0	3									
	Apr '22	952	0	0										
	May '22	995	0											
	Jun '22													
	Jul '22													
	Aug '22													

For accounts originated in Sep '21, Jun '22 is 9 months since origination. However, for accounts originated in Mar '22, Jun '22 is 3 months since origination.

Count of accounts that meet the delinquency definition, based on months since origination.

Count of new accounts originated each month from your observation data.

Figure 6 Shows the vintage analysis updated with the performance information

The vintage analysis report

Once all this information is collected, we can build the vintage report and the associated chart. The vintage report shows either the number, or more often, the proportion of accounts that meet the performance definition. These are expressed as a percentage of the number of accounts that originated in each tranche.

Vintage Analysis (2+ Cycles Delq)		Months since Origination											
		1	2	3	4	5	6	7	8	9	10	11	12
Origination Month	Sep '21	0.00%	0.00%	0.30%	0.40%	1.21%	1.51%	2.31%	2.92%	5.23%			
	Oct '21	0.00%	0.00%	0.31%	0.41%	1.22%	1.53%	2.24%	3.05%				
	Nov '21	0.00%	0.00%	0.20%	0.20%	0.98%	1.28%	1.77%					
	Dec '21	0.00%	0.00%	0.31%	0.31%	1.35%	1.55%						
	Jan '22	0.00%	0.00%	0.31%	0.41%	1.12%							
	Feb '22	0.00%	0.00%	0.40%	0.40%								
	Mar '22	0.00%	0.00%	0.30%									
	Apr '22	00.0%	0.00%										
	May '22	0.00%											
	Jun '22												
	Jul '22												
	Aug '22												

Figure 7 Vintage analysis report

The vintage analysis chart

The chart shows the same result, visually. It is sometimes easier to identify concerning trends using a chart.

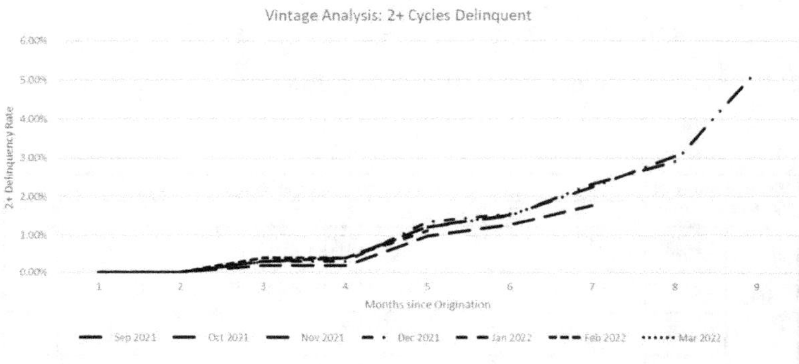

Figure 8 Vintage analysis chart

We can see that accounts that originated more recently have fewer associated performance months. That makes sense because less time has elapsed.

The chart shows the power of the vintage analysis. Looking at the chart, we can see that performance for the November 2021 tranche looks better than the other tranches (the 2+ delinquency rates for Nov 2021 are lower than the other tranches).

Based on this, it would be worth understanding what happened in Nov 2021. Is this seasonal? Did we do something differently at the point of origination to ensure that lower-risk accounts were approved?

Alternative vintage analysis chart

While this is how vintages are usually measured, there is another way to look at them. The same data is prepared in the same way, but it is visualised differently.

In the case below, the 2+ delinquency rates after six months are shown in the chart. Again, we see that the Nov 2021 tranche outperforms the Sep, Oct and Dec 2021 tranches.

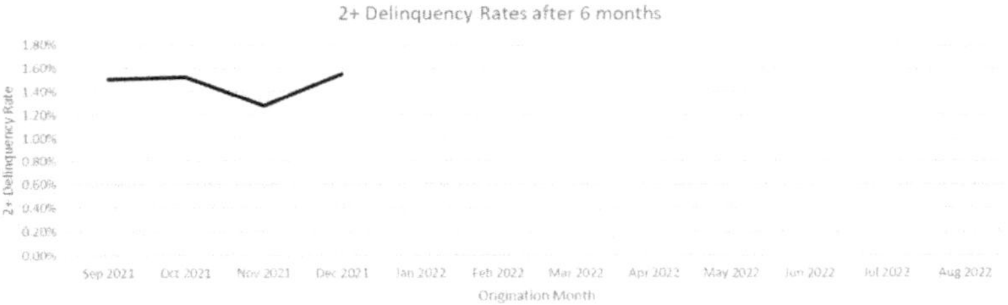

Figure 9 An alternative way of visualising vintages

302: Joint odds matrix

A joint odds matrix comprises two metrics, and account performance observed within the cells is used to classify similar cells for similar treatments. Cells are grouped based on the GBOdds (performance) observed. Typically, we use two scores (say, application and bureau scores), but any two metrics can be used.

A joint odds matrix, used at the point of account origination, is a highly effective way of ensuring that the credit bureau score is considered without using the credit bureau score as a characteristic within the application scorecard. Some organisations include the credit bureau score; however, this is not my preferred approach.

Reasons not to include bureau scores as a characteristic within the application scorecard

1. If the scorecard starts underperforming and the issue lies with the credit bureau score, you will need a scorecard developer to either adjust or rebuild your scorecard.
2. Scorecard development is an extremely specialised skillset and is typically expensive.

3. This will involve bringing in external consultants unless you have an internal scorecard development team.

4. Once the scorecard has been reweighted or rebuilt, it will need to be implemented. Scorecard implementations can be IT resource intensive and may be delayed or deferred due to a lack of resources.

5. If you switch primary bureau, you will incur costs to obtain the score used as a characteristic, as it is unlikely that you can substitute one bureau score for another without reweighting the characteristic (see previous points).

I've seen many application scorecards with bureau scores embedded in them. It suggests that a very influential scorecard developer must have worked for a bureau and promoted this inclusion. My view? Don't include bureau scores as a scorecard characteristic.

> **Don't include bureau scores as a scorecard characteristic.**

Reasons to build a joint odds matrix

1. If you decide to switch primary bureau supplier, there is no need to redevelop your scorecard.

2. Credit risk analysts can (and should) be the team to develop or redevelop the joint odds matrix.

3. Testing a joint odds implementation is significantly less work than testing a scorecard implementation. That means the internal IT resources required are far less.

4. If the bureau redevelops its scorecard, there's no need to adjust yours; just recreate the joint odds matrix, see previous comments on IT resources and scorecard development resources.

Now let's look at how to build this wonderful joint odds matrix.

Observation data

We will need at least 12 months of applications (regardless of final decisions) to ensure that seasonality is included within the analysis.

Collect the following information for each application:

- application date
- application number
- account number (where applicable – typically accepted applications only)
- final decision on the application
- application score
- credit bureau score
- flag indicating whether the application was declined due to a policy rule (not a business rule).

Performance data

The performance window should be the same one used during application scorecard development. If using a different variable, I suggest at least 12 months of performance information per account.

We need to know the delinquency and balance outstanding at month-end for each account in each performance month. For credit card and revolving loan accounts, month-end is typically the statement date, whereas, for personal loans, it would typically be the account due date.

Once the data is available, we're ready to build the joint odds analysis.

Just as we 'normalised' (very different to how the word is used in SQL) the data for a vintage analysis, we want to do so here too. In effect, the performance months are identified as the number of months since the observation date for each account. The figure below shows an example of the observation month dates and associated performance month dates. As you can see from this example, you will need at least two years of data.

Dates	Performance Months											
Obs Month	1	2	3	4	5	6	7	8	9	10	11	12
January 2020	Feb 2020	Mar 2020	Apr 2020	May 2020	Jun 2020	Jul 2020	Aug 2020	Sep 2020	Oct 2020	Nov 2020	Dec 2020	Jan 2021
February 2020	Mar 2020	Apr 2020	May 2020	Jun 2020	Jul 2020	Aug 2020	Sep 2020	Oct 2020	Nov 2020	Dec 2020	Jan 2021	Feb 2021
March 2020	Apr 2020	May 2020	Jun 2020	Jul 2020	Aug 2020	Sep 2020	Oct 2020	Nov 2020	Dec 2020	Jan 2021	Feb 2021	Mar 2021
April 2020	May 2020	Jun 2020	Jul 2020	Aug 2020	Sep 2020	Oct 2020	Nov 2020	Dec 2020	Jan 2021	Feb 2021	Mar 2021	Apr 2021
May 2020	Jun 2020	Jul 2020	Aug 2020	Sep 2020	Oct 2020	Nov 2020	Dec 2020	Jan 2021	Feb 2021	Mar 2021	Apr 2021	May 2021
June 2020	Jul 2020	Aug 2020	Sep 2020	Oct 2020	Nov 2020	Dec 2020	Jan 2021	Feb 2021	Mar 2021	Apr 2021	May 2021	Jun 2021
July 2020	Aug 2020	Sep 2020	Oct 2020	Nov 2020	Dec 2020	Jan 2021	Feb 2021	Mar 2021	Apr 2021	May 2021	Jun 2021	Jul 2021
August 2020	Sep 2020	Oct 2020	Nov 2020	Dec 2020	Jan 2021	Feb 2021	Mar 2021	Apr 2021	May 2021	Jun 2021	Jul 2021	Aug 2021
September 2020	Oct 2020	Nov 2020	Dec 2020	Jan 2021	Feb 2021	Mar 2021	Apr 2021	May 2021	Jun 2021	Jul 2021	Aug 2021	Sep 2021
October 2020	Nov 2020	Dec 2020	Jan 2021	Feb 2021	Mar 2021	Apr 2021	May 2021	Jun 2021	Jul 2021	Aug 2021	Sep 2021	Oct 2021
November 2020	Dec 2020	Jan 2021	Feb 2021	Mar 2021	Apr 2021	May 2021	Jun 2021	Jul 2021	Aug 2021	Sep 2021	Oct 2021	Nov 2021
December 2020	Jan 2021	Feb 2021	Mar 2021	Apr 2021	May 2021	Jun 2021	Jul 2021	Aug 2021	Sep 2021	Oct 2021	Nov 2021	Dec 2021

Figure 10 Observation and performance data dates

When I prepare data for a joint odds analysis, I build it following the outline of this table. I keep the observation and performance data in a single dataset with the performance data variables renamed to indicate which performance month they are associated with, rather than their date. Note that observation data can be associated with a date because there is only one instance of observation data for each record.

Create analysis variables

Using the performance data, we can create a good/bad flag. This is based on the maximum delinquency on each account during the performance window. If your scorecard is one of the axes in the analysis, I recommend using the scorecard G/B definition.

Failing that, and depending on bad volumes, use a bad definition of max 3+, or 4+ cycles delinquent during the performance period.

If you're unsure which performance definition to use, use either of the following definitions.

Performance Definition	3+	4+
Bad	Max Delq = 3+	Max Delq = 4+
Indeterminate	Max Delq = 2	Max Delq = 3
Good	Max Delq = Only ever 0 or 1	Max Delq = Only ever 0, 1 or 2

Figure 11 Performance definition options

All records must be stamped with their good/bad flag. The final data set used in the joint odds analysis contains the following variables:

- application number
- account number
- final decision
- application score (or variable 1)
- credit bureau score (or variable 2)
- good/bad flag
- balance outstanding in month 12 (or final performance month).

Once this is gathered, you are ready to proceed with the analysis.

Coarse class scores

If using scores to build the joint odds matrix, now is the time to coarse class them. For this example, I will assume that you're using an application score and a credit bureau score.

What do I mean by coarse classing?

This is a technique used in scorecard development. In simple terms, we want to group scores that perform similarly together.

We apply a binning process to the scores to create fewer bins, typically five. It is essential to ensure there are sufficient goods and bads in all cells (a minimum of 25 of each in each cell).[26]

This is how you do it.

Create a dataset summarising the application score by score. Identify the quintiles, create a cumulative frequency of the number of records in each score and identify the first 20%, next 20% and so on until you have five groups.

Now create an application score coarse classed variable based on these groups.

Repeat this exercise with the credit bureau score.

Once you have the axes for your joint odds matrix, we can get into the nitty-gritty!

Preparing for joint odds analysis

I have always done this next part of joint odds matrix analysis in Excel using pivot tables, but you could use any application.

Create the following summaries and populate the associated cross tabs:

- Count of applications
- Count of accepted applications
- Accept rate (accepted applications/applications)
- Count of good accepted applications
- Count of bad accepted applications
- Sum of good balances
- Sum of bad balances
- GBOdds (good balances / bad balances).

Metric		**Credit Bureau Score**					Total
		Band 1	Band 2	Band 3	Band 4	Band 5	
Application Score	Band 1						
	Band 2						
	Band 3						
	Band 4						
	Band 5						
Total							

Figure 12 Cross-tab populated with each of the metrics

And now the fun begins!

Joint odds analysis – science meets art

This exercise aims to create risk grades that can be used at the point of origination to separate applications based on the risk they pose to the organisation. We want to auto-decline or auto-approve (subject to policy rules and affordability constraints) as many applications as possible. In addition, we want to identify which applications need intense underwriting and which may need underwriting to a lesser extent. All of these factors combine to ensure that we optimise operations resources.

And now the fun begins!

If we could apply hard and fast rules, this would all be science, and there would be no art, and no room for discussion. There are certainly guidelines that consider your organisation's risk appetite and understand the highest marginal risk your organisation is prepared to take. There are conversations around loss-leading policies and whether those might be on the table. These determine risk grades and how they are treated.

While it is impossible to cover every eventuality here, this section will give you solid guidance on creating an initial joint odds matrix and having discussions to determine what will be implemented.

Essentially, we want to create five risk grades.

Risk Grade 1 – Decline

Extremely high risk. These applications are automatically declined. If the applicant challenges the decision, it should only be overturned after careful consideration.

Risk Grade 2 – High risk

Very high risk and high risk. These applications are referred to the underwriting team for manual decisions. I would expect the final acceptance rate of these applications to be low; because underwriters cherry-pick the best of the bunch. You can expect reasonably good performance if your underwriters do an excellent job.

Risk Grade 3 – Medium risk

These applications are still fairly high risk and would be referred for some degree of underwriting, such as employer verification. The amount of underwriting applied to these is less intense than for high-risk applications. We want to balance the risk posed by this group of applicants with the operational costs associated with underwriting.

Risk Grade 4 – Low risk

As these applications are low risk, depending on having passed policy rules and affordability criteria, they are not subject to any underwriting and are automatically approved.

Risk Grade 5 – Very low risk

These applications are automatically approved, subject to policy rules and affordability.

The key difference between low and very low risk applicants is that more favourable terms and conditions can be offered to very low risk applicants.

Finalising the joint odds matrix

With the key metrics in the matrices and an understanding of the various risk bands, we can start creating the joint odds matrix.

There are overarching principles in play here: Where accept rates are high and performance is good – these cells are candidates for auto-approval. Where accept rates are high and performance is mediocre, these cells are candidates for some type of underwriting activity. The idea is to do as much manual intervention as is necessary and as little as possible to achieve the desired outcome.

There is no objective right or wrong answer.

Where accept rates are low and performance is poor, it may be worth considering whether applications in these cells ought to be declined outright.

There is no objective right or wrong answer. Your organisation's risk appetite and product strategy are vital in determining what level of risk you are prepared to accept.

Typically, this process involves an initial recommended matrix created by the risk analyst. This matrix is then reviewed and ratified by either the head of risk or the appropriate credit risk committee.

Metric		Credit Bureau Score				
		Band 1	Band 2	Band 3	Band 4	Band 5
Application Score	Band 1	D	D	D	HR	HR
	Band 2	D	HR	HR	HR	MR
	Band 3	D	HR	MR	MR	LR
	Band 4	HR	MR	MR	LR	VLR
	Band 5	HR	MR	LR	VLR	VLR

Figure 13 Joint odds matrix cell outcomes

The table in figure 13 shows a typical joint odds matrix pattern, with low-scoring applications declined as high risk and high-scoring applications treated as low or very low risk, with minimal interventions applied.

Once you have created your joint odds matrix, it is a good idea to create a summary table showing the number of applications and accepted applications in each risk band. You will then be able to calculate the accept rate and GBOdds (by balance) for each risk band.

It's worth pointing out that the accept rate and GBOdds will be a function of historical actions. Consider applying the accept rate and GBOdds observed for the historical risk bands to estimate the likely impact of the recommended joint odds matrix on your portfolio.

One more thing, before we move on from joint odds matrices...

When you rebuild your joint odds matrix (12-24 months later), you may find that the highest-risk applicants are performing well, and it may be tempting to reduce the recommended level of underwriting. When making these recommendations and decisions, make sure you consider the approval rate as well as the GBOdds.

If the approval rate is low and subsequent performance is good, it likely means that your underwriters were doing an exceptional job and cherry-picked the best from an otherwise bad bunch. If you reduce underwriting on that group of applicants, you may see a significant deterioration in subsequent performance.

Risk grades are useful for several reasons. You can use them to determine how much underwriting to complete on applications. Risk grades can also be used to set terms, such as minimum and maximum loan terms or credit limits, and to set annual interest rates. This is especially helpful if your organisation is impacted by adverse selection.

Risk grades mean you can utilise risk-based strategies with any number of actions without applying those actions to all applications or accounts.

303: What-if analysis

If you've been performing analytics for a while, you'll have been asked:

What will happen if...

- we reduce the application score and take on more risk?
- we don't underwrite this group of applications?
- we change credit reporter?
- we participate in CCR (comprehensive credit reporting in New Zealand)?

Analysts use what-if analysis to determine the impact of pulling various levers as this helps increase understanding of the dynamics and dependencies. It is also known as simulation or sensitivity analysis.[27] Excel has built-in functionality that enables what-if analysis.

In the world of credit risk analytics, we use what-if analysis to understand the likely impact of changes to strategies on the outcomes. We typically focus on two key metrics.

The first is the metric we're trying to influence – for example, accept rate, balance build, spend or interest earned. The second is the impact of our strategy changes on bad debts.

Bad debts are not necessarily limited to gross charge-off over the next 12 months. They could include changes in arrears, changes in delinquency profile and impact on provisions.

By quantifying the impact on the targeted metric and the effect on bad debts, we can share a more complete and longer-term view of what will likely happen if the proposed change is implemented.

This could be important to your audience.

Let's consider an example

You're working through some analysis on the account originations strategy. Your primary objective is to increase the number of new accounts without adversely impacting the operational underwriting team. That means there is limited opportunity to increase the number of applications the operational team is expected to underwrite or review.

Given the metric criteria, you determine that converting some cells from medium to low risk means they will not be reviewed. This will free up operational resources to review the higher-risk cells. Not only will the accept rate increase for the medium-risk cells that have been reassigned, but fewer applications will automatically be declined. Therefore, overall, you will have more approved accounts. So far, so good?

Well, maybe.

To determine whether this will likely be all good, we need to estimate its possible impact on arrears. If these changes are expected to increase the number of accounts rolling into early stage arrears, we must weigh up whether the arrears team have the capacity to work these accounts. If they do, we could use current expectations to determine the likely impacts on gross charge-off, arrears, and, potentially, provisions. However, if the arrears team cannot manage the increased flow, we should expect to see an increased roll through arrears. Remember that if accounts are not rehabilitated early in arrears, the likelihood of rehabilitating them reduces as their delinquency increases.

It is also fair to say that the collective provisioning rate typically increases with increasing arrears. That means the increased roll through arrears is a double whammy, as provisions are expected to increase both because of the increased monetary value in arrears and because of the increased rate it is rolling through arrears.

To determine whether the change in the originations strategy is a good idea, we need to estimate the likely impact of these events. This will provide enough information to ensure a robust debate.

To my way of thinking, what-if analysis isn't prescriptive, as it doesn't indicate the best course of action. However, it is a useful way to unpack the potential up and downsides of a change. Assumptions should be robustly tested, and operational teams should be included in discussions and information gathering about any change that involves them.

Note that what-if analysis is different from prescriptive analytics, which is used to determine the best course of action.

> **Robust what-if analysis isn't just nice to have.**

Credit risk analysis is an important piece of the puzzle, but we do not operate in a vacuum. Our actions impact operational teams, marketing strategies and the bottom line of our organisations. Robust what-if analysis isn't just nice to have, it is essential if we are to add value to the broader organisation.

304: Recovery curves

Recovery curves are used to understand the impact of post-gross charge-off activity. At the point of gross charge-off, a few things happen:

- Any provisions held on the account are released (as the loss has been realised).
- No further interest or fees are applied to the account, so the balance can only reduce as payments occur.
- In unsecured retail consumer risk, gross charge-off is most common when the account has become seven cycles in arrears, regardless of when the most recent payment was made.
- Any payments made to the account after the point of charge-off are considered recoveries.

Many years ago, when working for a financial services organisation, our team was tasked with understanding the best course of action for accounts that had been charged-off. (This is often what a high-level problem statement looks like to senior credit risk analysts.) It was up to us to unpack what was required.

In this case, we needed to evaluate several options.

Option 1: Use the in-house recovery team exclusively to recover debt.

Option 2: Use external recovery collection agencies to recover debt.

Option 3: Sell debt that could be sold.

Option 4: Some combination of the above.

The key caveat was to maximise the amount recovered while maintaining the ability to conduct robust A/B testing (whilst obviously complying with company policy and applicable regulations). That last part, in brackets, should be implicit, but it helps define the legislative requirements and obligations, so everyone is clear on what may or may not be done. It helps to have these things well-articulated and documented so that the appropriate committees and interested parties are confident that all is in order.

As always, we ask, 'What does good look like?' In this case, the best outcome maximised net recoveries. To understand what those looked like, we must work out the recoveries.

Recovery curves are built like vintage curves. We know when the account was charged-off, and any payments received after that date are deemed a recovery. We add those payments and track cumulative payments over time.

Repayment curves can, and usually are, expressed in two ways:

- The total payments received over time.
- The total payments received over time, expressed as a percentage of the amount charged-off.

Observation data

From an observation perspective, we need all the relevant information about the account at the point of charge-off. That includes the date, amount, recovery score (if available) and bureau score (if available). It could also include other variables such as days since last payment, broken promises to pay (PTPs) past six months, PTPs kept past six months, number of payments made past month, three months, six months, 12 months, block code etc. Essentially, we want to create a dataset containing all the information known about the account at the point of gross charge-off.

Performance data

From a performance data point of view, we want to gather all payments received on the account, the dates those payments were received, and information about which agency is collecting the debt (in-house or external). For debt collected internally, it may be helpful to know whether we have strong recovery agents (although this would only apply if accounts are assigned to particular agents).

Analysing recovery curves

Once we have the data, we can start analysing it. I find it useful to understand what the overall picture looks like by tranche of charged-off debt. To do this, look at the total amount and the number of accounts charged-off each month, then chart the cumulative recovery amount.

Here are some key things to look out for:

- Do you see high levels of gross charge-off in some months? Is something seasonal going on?
- Is the average charged-off amount consistent, or do you see months where the average is higher or lower than expected? If so, why? What is driving this?
- If a higher than average number of records and amounts are being charged-off, ring fence that group of accounts to understand the driving forces behind them.

When the data is in and reshaped, you can calculate the amount and percentage recovered in the months post gross charge-off, then start building your curves. You want to know the shape of the curve. Typically, more money is collected earlier, and it tapers off over time. Once recovery curves flatten, you can see that continued effort does not drive continued payments received.

It is useful for the internal team to recognise when collecting on these accounts is no longer cost-effective. Essentially, you're estimating the incremental cost of collections against the incremental payments received. Perhaps this is debt that ought to be sold?

A word on team productivity

A word of warning: It is tempting to get deep into detail here, especially when attributing costs. I think a back-of-the-envelope calculation is good enough, especially if you have limited team resources. Remember, every minute you're doing thing A, you're not doing thing B or C. The incremental benefit obtained by spending weeks (or months!) refining the profit calculation is unlikely to outweigh the benefits derived from resolving this issue and moving on to the next important piece of work.

Now, back to the recovery curve analysis.

Once you've established whether there are any funnies or outliers in terms of average charge-off amounts and you have a good idea about the average shape of your overall recovery curve, it's time to start digging into things.

I start by comparing performance across in-house and external recovery agencies. It is important to understand whether they're all on an even playing field. Are the accounts given to one external agency interchangeable with accounts given to another? If the answer is yes, then you can measure the relative success of agencies based on recovery rates.

Another word of warning: If you assign 10% of accounts/balances to one agency, observe that they outperform their competitor(s) and give them 90% of accounts/balances the following period, you may notice a reversal of fortunes. Your champion recovery agency may suddenly be your worst performer. When this happens, we tend to ask what happened!

In simple terms, the wunderkind recovery agency managed the smaller volumes well and may have worked them hard and frequently. With the dramatic increase in volumes, they don't necessarily have levels of staff who can apply the same level of attention to accounts, so their performance drops off. Not only does your organisation not realise the expected recovery benefits, but it may also develop a reputation for creating havoc for suppliers.

One of the key reasons we were tasked with the piece of analysis mentioned earlier, was because the external collections and recovery agencies were unimpressed with how accounts had been divided up. It all came to a rather messy head when the COO berated previous star performers for underperforming, and the previous underperformers were suddenly star performers.

Businesses cannot scale up and down like yoyos. While being competitive is great, building solid relationships with suppliers and working with them when results do not meet expectations is infinitely more useful. The alternative, creating an environment where we alienate our suppliers and create environments where individuals and companies are set up to fail, doesn't end well.

305: Estimating gross charge-off using Markov chains

What's the (bad debt) number?

This phrase is commonly heard around month-end when everyone anxiously waits for financial numbers to be published. It refers to the final net charge-off for the month, which can include the gross charge-off and recoveries and movement in the provision.

I worked for a company that placed huge focus on the bottom-line impact each month. This included the gross charge-off, recoveries and the impact on provisions and was a bit of a moving feast. It was further complicated by the fact that the charge-off definition included a recency component (when a customer had last made a qualifying payment, not just how many cycles in arrears they were).

> What a risk team does, in terms of settings and strategies, directly impacts losses.

Unsurprisingly, the credit team also focussed on the impact on the bottom line. Losses impact a company's profitability and should be everyone's concern, not just the finance team's.

What a risk team does, in terms of settings and strategies, directly impacts losses. What marketing teams do and who they attract also affect losses (although in a slightly less direct line). It's the same for operational teams.

'If you cannot measure something, you cannot manage it', is the maxim attributed to leadership legend Peter Drucker.[28]

I'm not talking about measuring something that has already happened. We're not measuring losses; we're measuring past performance and using those results to estimate future losses and inform conversations, discussions and decisions.

Losses

This is a BIG topic.

It gets a lot of face time with a lot of important people (think CFOs, COOs, CEOs and sometimes the board).

I've lost track of the number of robust (corporate speak for unpleasant and confrontational) conversations I've had on this topic. Why do these conversations get so thorny? In my view, it's because profits are down and bonuses evaporate if losses are too high. Reducing the losses usually means introducing something that isn't currently happening, and there are often costs involved in getting that right. The other issue is that it can be difficult to turn late-stage collections around. And that is why I believe every organisation should have a robust way of estimating likely gross charge-offs that can signal, sooner rather than later, that trouble is brewing and they need to act.

A little less shooting the messenger would be pretty cool too.

When I was a credit risk analyst for a large financial services company, the financial year end was approaching, which meant we were tasked with budgets for the following year. Our team was asked to estimate the likely bad debts. As always, there were time pressures, and two of my colleagues were off work. I prepared my analysis and double-checked it.

> **A little less shooting the messenger would be pretty cool too.**

I knew the CFO and the COO were unlikely to be thrilled with the news. My analysis showed that, given the expected macro conditions, if we did more of what we were currently doing, we should expect a significant increase in losses the following year.

The CFO was not happy. He stood up, leaned over the desk and yelled.

The COO was not happy. He did not yell, but he also thought the numbers were highly implausible.

And that is the nature of future estimates, even when they are based on past performance. From my point of view, the yelling wasn't likely to change the outcome; it would take doing something differently to change the future.

This example shows so many things that were not done well. Analysts need to learn to manage these kinds of conversations if they want to be more than senior analysts. I've learned those hard lessons. At that first trial-by-fire meeting, the CFO's reaction took me by surprise, but it provided many opportunities for growth and learning. Over the years, I've had similar conversations with CFOs, CROs and CEOs. The conversations are never fun, but there is a way to deliver the message so that it lands and triggers appropriate action and steps to avert significant losses.

Markov chains are a way of using the current experience of how accounts move through current transition matrices, to step through a specified number of months and estimate future results.

Building Markov chains

To build Markov chains, you will need transition matrices, which we discussed in Module 2 (203). I recommend you brush up if you're not yet across these.

Transition matrices are the foundation for the Markov chain we'll be building to estimate the likely gross charge-off.

There is plenty of literature on Markov chains and Monte Carlo simulations and quite a bit of talk about stochastic processes and discrete and continuous time. Basically, you can use lots of big, important, scary-sounding words.[29] As a side note: I've known analysts who do this to sound clever. It's the analytical equivalent of name-dropping; I'm not a fan. In my opinion, the best analysts can explain something complex and with far-reaching implications so that non-technical people understand what is happening.

Back to Markov chains.

We know that account performance is seasonal, and delinquency rates tend to deteriorate post-Christmas, before improving again. Given that, I prefer to use 12 months of transition matrix history to create an average matrix.

> The best analysts can explain something complex and with far-reaching implications so that non-technical people understand what is happening.

Here's a key question: Should this matrix be a simple average of the rates? Or should the average rate be calculated as a weighted function of the balances that transition? I usually use the balances, then create and use the weighted transition rates.

But (of course, there must be a but), if your portfolio is growing (or shrinking) rapidly, I would consider using the simple average of the rates. The weighted average would skew the rates towards the time when overall balances were larger. This is where science meets art, and good judgement is required.

To estimate likely gross charge-off using Markov chains, the transition matrix needs to be square (more on this in a moment). That means we make a few minor modifications to the transition matrix.

The principles are identical – we want to know where the accounts were last month and this month.

We also want to include any pertinent closed states (which is a state that an account can enter but cannot leave). For example, accounts can become more or less delinquent based on payments, or lack thereof. Therefore, levels of delinquency are not closed states. However, once an account has been charged-off, it cannot be un-charged-off, so gross charge-off and closed accounts tend to be closed states used in Markov chains.

Accounts cannot leave closed states, so the final two rows in the table (figure 14) seem unnecessary but are required for the chain. However, we know that all accounts that were charged off are still in the same state, and all accounts that were in a closed state last month are still closed.

Transition Matrix		Delinquency this month								
		UTD	Delq1	Delq2	Delq3	Delq4	Delq5	Delq6	GCO	Closed
Delinquency last month	UTD	😊😊😊	🙁						🙁	😖
	Delq1	😊😊😊	😐	🙁					🙁	😖
	Delq2	😊😊😊	🙂	😐	🙁				🙁	😖
	Delq3	😊😊😊	🙂	🙂	😐	🙁			🙁	😖
	Delq4	😊😊😊	🙂	🙂	🙂	😐	🙁		🙁	😖
	Delq5	😊😊😊	🙂	🙂	🙂	🙂	😐	🙁	🙁	😖
	Delq6	😊😊😊	🙂	🙂	🙂	🙂	🙂	😐	🙁	😖
	GCO								🙁	
	Closed									😖

Figure 14 The transition matrix used in Markov chains to estimate likely gross charge-off

As you can see, we now have a 9x9 matrix.

Using Marcov chains to estimate likely gross charge-off in 12 months

To estimate gross charge-off in 12 months, you will need to do the following:

1. Create your average transition matrix based on the most recent 12 transition matrices (13 months of data), including the closed states that apply to your portfolio and organisation.

2. Ensure that your transition matrix is populated with rates, and remember that the rates are based on row totals.

3. Make sure it is a square matrix (as many rows as there are columns). In order to estimate the likely gross charge-off in 12 months' time, we need to multiply the matrix by itself 12 times.

4. Use linear algebra to multiply this matrix together 12 times. This will result in a transition matrix that is populated with rates. We're interested in the final gross charge-off rates.

5. Create a summary of balances by delinquency profile (current month) and multiply these balances (by level of delinquency) by the estimated gross charge-off by level of delinquency. This will give the estimated amount likely to be charged off in 12 months' time, based on the account's current level of delinquency. This is illustrated in the table in figure 15.

6. Sum the estimated gross charge-off, and divide that by the sum of the current balances, and this will give you the estimated gross charge-off rate. In the example below, we've estimated that 6.25% of balances today will be charged off in 12 months' time.

	Balance	x Est GCO Rate	x Est GCO
Delq Profile	Balance	Est GCO Rate	Est GCO (in 12 months' time)
UTD	2,000,000	1.50%	30,000
Delq 1	250,000	10.00%	25,000
Delq 2	125,000	20.00%	25,000
Delq 3	50,000	40.00%	20,000
Delq 4	37,500	65.00%	24,375
Delq 5	25,000	80.00%	20,000
Delq 6	12,500	95.00%	11,875
	2,500,000	**6.25%**	**156,250**

Figure 15 Using the output of the Markov chain to estimate future gross charge-off

Estimate expected gross charge-off over the upcoming 12 months

In figure 15, the first column shows the delinquency profiles we're using. The second column shows the balances outstanding by level of delinquency, which ought to be readily available from your monthly reporting. The third column shows the estimated gross charge-off rate, which is sourced from the final transition matrix in the Markov chain. The fourth column shows the estimated gross charge-off amount, calculated by multiplying the balance outstanding for a particular level of delinquency by its corresponding estimated gross charge-off rate. These amounts are summed to give an overall estimated gross charge-off amount likely to be incurred over the coming 12 months.

It is useful to express this as a percentage of the balance outstanding as it will give you an idea of whether the estimated charge-off over the coming 12 months is likely to be higher or lower than is currently experienced.

In principle, this is relatively straightforward. We estimate the proportion of the current receivables likely to reach gross charge-off over the upcoming 12 months, by using the recent (previous 12 months) performance observed on the portfolio.

While having an estimated gross charge-off over the upcoming 12 months is useful, it's even more valuable to understand why the number is likely to be what it is. Using transition matrices also make the pain points visible. By identifying performance that needs improving, we can devise and implement specific strategies.

Typically, we can make the most impact in early-stage arrears. Understanding how the accounts transition month in and month out, means we can work with various operational teams and finance for the best opportunity to influence the results.

306: Sample size

Whenever the conversation turns to forecasts, people ask (quite reasonably) whether the results are valid. Sometimes they ask about confidence intervals, although after more than 25 years of working in credit risk, I've only once been asked about these, and that was by someone who didn't understand a weighted average.

Of course, there is a place for confidence intervals. However, in the day-to-day, when we're making decisions and confident that the results are robust and valid, we're comfortable taking it from there, looking at averages (weighted averages), standard deviations and reasonableness.

What is reasonable?

Reasonableness is a messy word, open to interpretation. But at the end of the day, you need to be able to explain why you're making particular recommendations, and no amount of: 'H_0 failed to be rejected at the 95th confidence interval' will change that. As analysts, our job is to break down what is going on. And that is best done by leaving the weird academic speak where it belongs, in academia.

> Reasonableness is a messy word, open to interpretation.

It's a Risky Business

Here's a funny story. When I was completing my master's degree, we had to do a starter course in econometrics. Our lecturer was adamant that we needed to phrase our results in a particular way for the answer to be deemed correct. I have never seen sentences like those we had to write in a business context. In business, it is best to ensure that your statements are clear and concise.

To ensure that our results are robust, valid and repeatable, we apply common sense and rules of thumb, courtesy of our academic and statistically-minded friends.

Again, plenty of literature talks about results being valid and repeatable. Unsurprisingly, in many cases, we want to be able to check that the results are, in fact, the results. Hans Plesser has written an excellent paper discussing the terminology, a bit of history and the context.[30] In a nutshell, there are semantic arguments involved. From a credit risk analyst's point of view, we must be able to repeat our analysis and be confident that we're sharing actionable insight with senior leaders and stakeholders.

That means we need to understand the business, not just the analytics. It's a tad embarrassing when you present your findings and someone in ops points out that they don't have the resources to execute, or someone in legal points out that whatever you're aiming to do doesn't comply with legislation.

Our numbers need to be statistically valid. The last thing you and your team want to do is raise alarm bells, only to discover that your sample size is so small that what you're suggesting is anecdotal. There is definitely a place for this as it's often what the ops people see and share. Analysts, though, need to look at the data and understand what is happening.

The central limit theorem is our friend when it comes to sample size.[31] The most important takeaway is that you want a sample size of at least 30 records. I'm willing to declare that if most of your cells/samples have at least 30 accounts in each category (typically good or bad, and a handful of cells have fewer of one or the other), that's OK. Again, art meets science.

That does not mean you *only* need 30 records to do your analysis!

It means you want *at least* 30 goods and *at least* 30 bads in each cell when you build a joint odds matrix. I must admit if I have several thousand records in a cell, and 25 are bad and the rest are good, I tend to be OK with that. Five more bads will not make me want to decline all the records. It also means that if I have 15 bads and 25 goods, I cannot meaningfully draw conclusions about the performance of that cell. Twenty-eight goods to 15 bads, gives GBOdds of 1.8 to 1. But if one of those wasn't really a bad, the odds would be 2 to 1, and if I had a few more bads, my odds would start dropping quite quickly. Basically, both the good and bad volumes are too low to draw valid, robust results.

How to ensure your work is robust, valid and repeatable

1. Have at least 30 goods and 30 bads per cell (or 'decision'). Otherwise, you risk whatever you implement

going sideways. Not only will this adversely impact the business and financials, but it is also unlikely to earn you a stellar reputation as an analyst.

2. Document what you're doing and why you're doing it. This could be added lines of commentary in your code. It could also be a how-to guide (useful when mitigating key person risk). The bottom line? Make sure what you're doing is known and understood outside your head.

3. Understand the business. That means chatting to the ops people on the ground. What do they see? Will your proposals make their lives more difficult, or are you helping them? What about legislation and regulatory compliance? And for that matter, what are the likely downstream impacts on ops and other teams?

307: Assessing the impact of policy and business rules

Policy and business rules usually feature in account originations. I distinguish between the two in the following way:

Policy rules ensure that we meet compliance and regulatory expectations. For example, we decline all applications where the applicant is less than 18 years old, as no one under this age can legally sign a contract.

We impose business rules to frame and meet our organisation's risk appetite. An example of a business rule? Refer all applications where the applicant is less than 21 years old.

In most businesses, if an application triggers a decline rule, it is declined, regardless of any other information. In some businesses, these applications are stopped the first time they trigger a decline rule, so no further rules are activated. In other businesses, an application will complete the process and be declined at the end. The key difference is the amount of data collected.

When conducting business rule effectiveness, we typically analyse those applications that trigger one or more *business* rules but no *policy* rules. It is often worth separating accounts that only trigger refer rules from those that trigger at least one decline rule, as these will have been automatically declined.

Creating a dataset for analysis

To evaluate the performance of business rules, we need to create an appropriate dataset. As discussed in Module 201, we need observations and performance over a period. Unlike building an entire originations strategy, we don't want all the applications, just those that triggered at least one refer rule and no policy decline rules within the observation window. Typically, we want at least 12 months of data in our observation window, to ensure we have accounted for seasonality.

Always take seasonality into consideration.

We want to know the final accept/decline decisions for all those applications and their associated good/bad flags. That means we need at least 12 months of performance data per approved account.

> Always take seasonality into consideration.

The purpose of this analysis is to ensure that business rules deliver effective outcomes. All referred applications must be reviewed and underwritten. Therefore, the settings must ensure that only applications that need to be, are reviewed.

One application can trigger multiple refer rules, which means that you may have a dataset with duplicate application numbers.

Key considerations

1. Are multiple business rules regularly triggered together? If you're seeing this, it warrants further analysis.
2. Where multiple rules are triggered together, consider the applications that only trigger one or two of the multiple rules. What does their performance look like? And how does that compare to applications that trigger the full combination of rules?
3. What does individual business rule performance look like? It may be that certain business rules drive performance regardless of any other rules triggered.

Note that, because we're analysing business rule performance, you will likely see the same application evaluated several times. This is not an issue, provided you have done the work to determine whether rules should be combined. In instances where you want to evaluate the performance of rules 1, 2 and 3, you should only have one instance of each application, and each should have triggered all three rules.

I prefer to create separate datasets to evaluate the rules. I do this for two key reasons.

1. It is totally transparent. I can tell exactly which business rule, or collection of rules, I'm evaluating.
2. I can loop through the code – essentially, I write one piece of code and then apply it to the various datasets.

All outputs can be attributed to the datasets they refer to, and I can review all results in one sitting.

As with the joint odds matrix, we need to ensure that we have at least 30 goods and 30 bads per business rule or business rule grouping being evaluated.

We evaluate the following key metrics:

- the number of applications that trigger the rule
- the number of applications that are subsequently approved
- approval rate
- the number of goods and bads
- GBOdds.

Common outcomes and how to treat them

Where the number of applications is exceptionally low, decide whether, for that specific rule, it is worth extracting a longer observation period. Without sufficient observations, it is impossible to make anything other than a judgement call. That's not necessarily a bad thing; you just need to ensure that the context and any assumptions are well understood.

> Ensure that the context and any assumptions are well understood.

Where a large number of applications trigger the business rules, and the subsequent approval rate is very low, you may want to consider auto-declining all applications that trigger this rule – even if the subsequent performance looks good. The reason for doing so is the costs involved in the underwriting versus the revenues from the subsequently approved accounts.

Where there are very high approval rates and the performance is satisfactory, consider removing or modifying the business rule, so that applications that perform well aren't flagged for review, and those that don't perform well, are. This is done by comparing the approved and declined applications and determining whether there are key themes or differences. You would also look at the approved and poorly performing accounts to decide whether or not they can be separated from the better performing records.

There are a couple of ways to do this. Brute force reviews all observation variables to see whether you can separate good and bad performing accounts. See if that makes sense when comparing applications that were approved with those that were declined. Alternatively, a correlation matrix will highlight which variables are strongly correlated, either positively or negatively, and you can use this to inform your analytics. And finally, having spent time learning about your data through EDA and data validations and understanding what the ops team look at, use this information to inform your thinking about how best to segment these applications.

Business knowledge goes a long way to informing these conversations and understanding how the underwriting team interprets what they're seeing.

There are times when there is no way to separate those accounts that perform well from those that do not. This is when you know that the underwriters are doing their jobs well.

Always ask questions

- How many applications are 'a few'? What is the trade-off between increasing auto declines, approving additional applications and incurring the associated operational underwriting costs?
- What is a low approval rate?
- What is a high approval rate?
- What do good GBOdds look like?

Unfortunately, the answer is often, 'It depends'.

It depends on your organisation's risk appetite, on what is palatable and on what normal looks like. And that is why so many credit risk decisions are the convergence of science and art. Often there is no hard and fast rule that you can point to and say, 'Yep, that's it!'

> Unfortunately, the answer is often, 'It depends'.

308: Evaluating profitability

I am not talking about profitability modelling here. Actually, I'm not a huge fan of it. (Gasp! Shock! Horror!)

My issue with profitability modelling is that profitability is a function of revenues and costs, while revenues are a function of spend and interest. (Side note: In my opinion, revenues should not be a function of fees.)

On the other hand, costs are a function of what we do operationally and our collections activities, provisioning for doubtful debts and net charge-off. The more we choose to do, the greater the costs incurred. There is a trade-off, though. For example, by doing less in collections, our operational costs decrease. However, there is a risk that our delinquencies will increase, likely driving increased provisioning for doubtful debt costs and increased gross charge-off costs. Although increased gross charge-off costs are likely to result in increased recoveries, (reducing net charge-off costs) the increase in recoveries is unlikely to offset the increase in gross charge-off.

After controlling for affordability, higher-risk individuals tend to spend more and incur higher interest charges – leading to increased revenues. They also tend to miss more payments,

> In my opinion, revenues should not be a function of fees.

spend more time in collections, incur higher provisioning costs and higher net charge-off costs – all leading to increased costs.

I'm a huge fan of explicitly being able to pull levers. So, I prefer to include a risk score (which talks to the cost element of profit) and a revenue or spend score (which talks to the revenue element of profit).

That was all a bit of an aside. This section is really all about *evaluating* profitability rather than trying to predict it.

In simple terms, we know that profit is a function of revenues minus costs. Things are profitable when revenues exceed costs. The greater that margin, the more profitable things are.

Nothing in that statement should be a surprise, and it definitely isn't ground-breaking.

Yet I've had several conversations with CFO types who were less than thrilled about this conversation. They pointed to the P&L and said, 'Of course the company is profitable'. They thought I was wasting their time. But I'm not talking about the company's profitability. The P&L answers that question.

What I'm talking about is the profitability of decisions at the margin.

What are decisions at the margin?

Decisions at the margin are where we decide to approve an account at the high end of the risk that an organisation is willing to take on. These are often the risk versus reward conversations that happen between sales and risk, or sales and finance.

When I want to evaluate profitability, these are the decisions I want to examine.

Another example of this type of decision comes from extremely low-risk accounts. When performance is very good, interest revenue is low as these individuals tend to transact on a credit card and pay the balance in full each month. Or they make a large purchase, take advantage of the interest-free period and repay the full amount during that time.

> These are often the risk versus reward conversations.

Evaluating profitability

When evaluating profitability, I have tried the cost-based accountancy approach, where every cost is identified and attributed to an action. This effectively assigns all attributable costs and determines whether the account/cell/business rule is profitable. It is an excellent exercise if you have the time, resource and inclination, offering phenomenal insights into the business and where things may not be working as expected. But it is also very time-consuming and requires resource from several areas of the business.

An alternative method is understanding the cost of actions applied to applications and accounts. For example, we determine what costs are assigned for all applications referred for underwriting and use this in the profitability metric. While less accurate than the first method, this is a much shorter exercise, involving averages and less engagement from fewer people.

You're still assigning costs and revenues to applications and accounts. You're still determining whether the decisions at the margin are profitable. And if they're not profitable, you're still in a position to decide whether they make sense as a loss leader.

Why would you do one and not the other? Well, it depends on what you plan to do with that information. And it depends on your organisation's comfort with uncertainty. Again, there is no absolute right or wrong answer.

We evaluate profitability from a risk point of view for several reasons. We may want to know whether the sunk marketing costs make sense, given the number of new accounts and their subsequent performance. We may want to understand more detail about a high-risk tranche of business. Are all sales worth it? Is the business worth doing if we're generating sales that become delinquent and are charged off?

Could we make changes that would result in increased revenues or reduced costs? And would that mean a particular tranche of business now makes sense?

This is why we evaluate profitability, to find the areas at the margin that might not make sense and do something to turn them around.

Module 3: Points to ponder

This module brought together everything we've looked at in the previous modules and examined them from different angles. Once you understand how to do credit risk analytics, you can use any of the tools to analyse any situation or concern.

Here are some key questions to think about:

- Have I got sufficient goods and bads to ensure that my analysis is robust?
- Do my observation and performance windows line up?
- Who am I presenting this analysis to? What are their key concerns and interests?
- Aside from what the data tells me, what else do I know that may have influenced the outcomes driving this analysis?
- What do I expect to see from this analysis? And does the analysis line up with my expectations? If not, why not?
- Who can I check my assumptions with?
- What impact will the changes I'm proposing have on operational teams?
- What impact could the changes I'm proposing have on the bottom line?
- What strategic objectives does my analysis align with?

I can do retail consumer credit risk analytics, so what?

Things happen in the credit risk environment, and some aren't planned. Sometimes they're small; a process is modified, and something unexpected happens. It is quickly identified and easily rectified. If things are going to go awry, that's what you want.

But it's often more complex than that.

The most concerning whoopsie I've seen, with the furthest-reaching consequences, involved a system upgrade where the date format was incorrectly applied. Accounts were billed on two consecutive days, rather than on the same date for two consecutive months. From the customer's point of view, once we understood what had happened, we reversed the error and sent out apologies. However, from a data and analytics point of view, the effect was felt for years. As the error persisted in the data, the two impacted months had to be excluded from all and any future analytics.

It's a Risky Business

More often than not, an event (or events) outside your (or your organisation's) control will impact credit risk strategies. Take the global financial crisis (GFC), for example. The response was swift. Lending rules tightened as banking and financial services organisations became more conservative and applied stricter rules. The impacts were especially noticeable for personal loans and non-revolving lending products.

With a solid understanding of retail consumer credit risk analytics, you understand that the portfolio will start shrinking if the front end (originations) in personal loans is curtailed. It happens because not enough new lending is happening. The customer cannot draw down or make repeat purchases on an existing line of credit with fixed-term products. Once the initial loan is issued, one of two things can happen. Either the customer meets their obligations and repays the loan, or they don't. As good balances reduce to zero, the total outstanding balance reduces.

Because fewer new loans are written (with more conservative rules and criteria applied), overall balance growth may stall or even become negative, resulting in a shrinking portfolio. However, because of the prevailing economic conditions, delinquent balances may increase due to increased hardship experienced by customers. Even if delinquent balances don't increase in absolute terms, they are likely to increase relative to the overall portfolio balances. And this results in an increasing delinquency rate, as the proportion of delinquent balances increases relative to the overall portfolio balance.

That is when it is important for credit risk analysts to understand the impact that one area of the business may have on other areas. During the GFC, I worked for an organisation whose collections operations teams were unpopular because the 30+ and 90+ rates were higher than expected. There were two key drivers for this:

1. Changes and tightened lending rules strongly curtailed the new accounts approved through originations. Unfortunately, as the new balance growth reduced, the flow-on impact was not adequately factored into arrears performance.
2. In addition, customers appeared to choose to pay down their loans faster, which exacerbated the reducing denominator.
3. More people were experiencing hardship and could no longer meet their obligations. That meant collections volumes increased, which put pressure on the teams with more calls to make and manage.

This perfect storm led to more late-stage arrears and charge-offs. However, tightening lending at the front end was still the most appropriate decision.

I've also seen marketing teams target people who will never pass the company's policy rules. This ultimately results in a very poor customer experience and a significant waste of money. There is also reputational risk for the organisation, especially in this hyperconnected age.

A thorough understanding of credit risk means the analyst can connect the dots and highlight future concerns and implications of actions before they happen. Acquiring a gut feel for these things isn't magic or crystal-ball gazing. It is most often hard-won from working through challenging and unexpected events. It involves keeping an open mind and asking a lot of questions, especially when things get weird.

> A thorough understanding of credit risk means the analyst can connect the dots.

It can be more difficult to understand key drivers in large organisations, where multiple teams are responsible for account originations, account management and collections. That's unless there is a practice of working together, keeping everyone in the loop and openly sharing issues or concerns. Everyone is busy, yet it's critical to find or make time to build relationships and stay up to date with what's happening, especially when the unexpected happens.

A credit risk subject matter expert (SME) can draw on their deep and broad knowledge to help others see how seemingly unrelated events conspire to drive unexpected outcomes.

As an analyst with enough experience, you start to have a 'spidey sense' (as one of my colleagues described it). You look at reports and just know something isn't quite right. Sometimes the most frightening thing you can hear from an analyst is, 'Mmmmm, that's interesting...'. It's usually muttered quietly under their breath. And then they start digging.

Many years ago, I worked in a financial services organisation, where several things conspired to create a problem. My team was responsible for credit strategy and policy, but we didn't have ready access to raw data. And in those days, there was no data warehouse.

> **You start to have a 'spidey sense'.**

There were two analytics teams. One team reported to the marketing function, but they did more than just marketing analysis and reporting, as they were also responsible for reports to other business areas, including the collections team.

The other analytical function resided within the collections team. One of our portfolios was securitised, which meant we had to adhere to the credit policy and various covenants.

No doubt you're beginning to see that things got tricky. Reporting wasn't automated and didn't reside within a single function. The credit strategy and policy team relied on other teams for reporting and analysis work. Gross charge-off was manual, so a report was run at each month-end, and passed to the collections team, which actioned all gross charge-offs manually. To further complicate matters, the gross charge-off definition included a recency component. Effectively, an account needed to be a specified number of cycles delinquent and not have made a payment in a specified number of months before it qualified for gross charge-off.

The two stand-outs for me were the manual report generation and the requirement for manual gross charge-off. These were prime candidates for automation.

There was nothing obvious — other than my distinct unease about the slight but persistent uptick in very late stage arrears. The two analytics functions were both extremely busy, and because there was no obvious cause for concern, it was impossible to reprioritise work to investigate. In the end, the issue was uncovered after we pleaded for access to data and pulled some data ourselves.

It turned out that a date had not been updated in one of the reports. A simple human error could have led to a world of pain, where covenants were missed and bad things happened.

> There is no substitute for experience.

Spend enough time understanding and analysing your portfolio, and you'll develop this 'spidey sense'. There is no substitute for experience. You cannot learn it. But you can learn to ask the right questions. You can learn to recognise when things seem off. And you can learn to build relationships across multiple teams — especially with the people at the proverbial coal face.

Once you've mastered the key credit risk skills, you understand how credit risk analytics interacts with other areas of the business. That means you can intuitively anticipate the likely impacts across the portfolio. It also means that when the unexpected happens, you have a head start in identifying, understanding and mitigating the impacts.

Now what?

It's one thing to have the intuitive sense that comes with a deep and intrinsic knowledge of credit risk analytics. It's something entirely different to communicate that effectively to various people within the organisation. Vague mutterings as you dive into something that looks interesting may be tolerated or even encouraged if your direct line manager has a deep understanding and appreciation of your ability to get to the nitty-gritty.

However, strong skills are increasingly important, as you progress from 'someone clever who knows a lot of complicated stuff' to a trusted SME. You become the go-to person, known for their ability to produce solid analytics, pre-emptively highlight key concerns, and communicate them to non-SMEs.

What do I mean by strong skills? They're all the skills that have traditionally been called soft. To my way of thinking, there is nothing soft about them. Analysts are rewarded for thinking logically and analytically. For starting at the beginning and working through a problem. For diving into the detail and understanding how everything fits together.

These skills serve us well while we're honing our technical skills. Unfortunately, they do not serve us quite as well when speaking with other parts of the business. That does not mean the technical skills we spent so long acquiring are now useless. Rather, we need to develop and hone a complementary set of skills to ensure we can connect meaningfully and communicate with parts of the business with different primary concerns.

Retail consumer credit risk analytics touches all areas of financial services. The rules and strategies we implement at account originations can render marketing activity redundant or less effective than expected. Some schools of thought say it's marketing's problem, but I do not share that philosophy. We all work for the same organisation, so we should work together to find solutions, rather than work at cross purposes.

> **Retail consumer credit risk analytics touches all areas of financial services.**

This philosophy holds true across all areas of the business. What we do in the credit risk world impacts the bottom line in many ways, across revenues, sales, charge-offs and provisions. Similarly, what we do affects operations. How we show up and lead our teams contributes to team and company culture.

These non-technical skills and concerns may not be the primary concern of the up-and-coming analyst, but I think they ought to be top of mind for all analysts who aspire to lead teams, either as an SME, a team lead, or beyond.

Almost every analyst who made the leap to team manager has shared stories of trial by fire. It turns out people think differently, and what's important to us, as analysts, may not even make the top ten things that are important to our stakeholders.

Developing and honing your skills is a crucial next step.

> # Developing and honing your skills is a crucial next step.

As you're doing so, it's time to decide which direction you want to head.

Do you want to become the ultimate technical expert? If so, continue with your explorations, and become a deep technical expert in all the systems, processes and business areas adjacent to credit risk analytics. These include originations, collections and customer service, and all the systems used. These generate data, (usually lots of it) and your analytical skills and deep understanding of credit risk will add depth, flavour, nuance and insight that other analysts (without your credit risk expertise) lack.

Do you want to be an SME leading projects? Then continue building relationships with people across your organisation in technical areas and operations. It pays to keep the customer front and centre, so build close working relationships with marketing and sales. Work with your direct line manager to engage in and lead projects that benefit from strong credit risk technical skills. Bring your skill set to the project so you can drive change that facilitates growth objectives, whilst mitigating risks and losses. The finance team will appreciate that.

Do you want to become a team lead, with your own team of credit risk analysts? In that case, focus on mentoring your junior colleagues. Help non-credit-risk experts meet their objectives and drive change. Demonstrate your team leadership and work with your line manager to identify opportunities.

There are many areas a credit risk analyst could move into, depending on your objectives. As individuals, we grow and learn, and by sharing that knowledge with our teams through coaching, mentoring and team discussions, we learn which elements strike a chord and what we want to explore next. We also discover areas for growth. Often, the key characteristics that serve us well as analysts no longer do so as we move into broader roles.

For example, analysts are expected and encouraged to play deep in the detail. It is difficult to produce great analytics without that ability, as something unexpected always seems to happen! However, as we step up, we're expected to see the big picture and think strategically, which can be very challenging.

If we only ever meet and relate to analysts, or other left-brain dominant types, suddenly working with people who think fundamentally differently and have different challenges and objectives can be hugely frustrating.

People are at the heart of all of this. They always have been. As junior analysts, we're often shielded from how tricky this can be.

It's a Risky Business

One day, we're suddenly expected to know all these things. This rite of passage is easier for some than others.

Retail consumer credit risk analytics plays a crucial role in financial services organisations.

Done well, it drives change leading to increased profitability, increased revenues through increased spend and interest yield, increased productivity and increased synergies between teams.

Done poorly, it still drives change, but unfortunately, this can result in increased arrears, leading to increased gross charge-off and collective provisions. Although the absolute value of recoveries may seem higher, net losses are still higher than they ought to be. Poor risk analytics can also produce less than optimal outcomes in operations teams, as they action applications and accounts that could be treated with a lighter touch or automatically actioned.

World-class credit risk analytics teams constantly look for ways to refine their strategies. They respond to the macroeconomic conditions and to callouts from operational teams who see things at the coal face. World-class teams know there is always room for improvement. There are always opportunities to refine activity, increase efficiencies, and improve the experience for internal operational teams and the customer.

Credit risk managers know that their teams can and do add value. They look for projects to stretch and grow their team members in ways that serve the individuals. All this whilst ensuring that the analytics they deliver drive increased profitability through increased revenues or reduced costs and increased operational efficiencies without compromising the quality of the risk decisions.

World-class credit risk analysts don't come out of universities; they are shaped and informed by their environments, especially as junior to mid-level analysts. These early environments set them up for later success. This investment ensures they have a solid understanding of the basics and appreciate the subtleties of credit risk analytics. It is repaid in spades as they mature into senior analysts.

Credit risk analysts are fluent in the language of credit risk. They have more than a detailed understanding of the fundamental principles of analytics. They have a thorough understanding of the first principles of conducting robust, valid and repeatable analytics and can apply these skills to any number of situations. This ability to extract meaningful insight from the data and understand how to leverage it to deliver bottom-line benefits sets leading SMEs apart from the rest.

As a credit risk analyst, do you have a detailed understanding of the principles described in this book? Do you truly know how to apply and leverage them to drive change for your organisation?

I have spent many years developing and honing my credit risk technical skills and helping other credit risk analysts develop theirs. My focus is on mentoring credit risk teams and analysts, ensuring that the newest generation of analysts have these skills at the ready and can continue to drive change in their organisations.

About the author

Carolyn Röhm is creative, innovative, logical and analytical in equal measure, with a strong focus on driving change that aligns with business objectives. Her expertise covers the full spectrum of consumer lending. Carolyn adds value by developing and implementing all aspects of credit risk strategies, maximising revenues while minimising losses.

She has extensive experience in account origination strategies, limit management strategies, and early and late-stage collections strategies. Her focus is on customer rehabilitation and, where that is not possible, recovery maximisation.

Carolyn has spent more than 20 years working in banks and financial services organisations in South Africa and New Zealand, with responsibilities in Australia. In South Africa, she worked with financial services organisations and banks, including HomeChoice, Woolworths Financial Services and PIC Solutions. At PIC Solutions, Carolyn worked on projects for clients including

Truworths, ABSA Bank, Boland Bank, The Forshini Group and Edcon.

In 2008 Carolyn and her family moved to Wellington, New Zealand, and then to Auckland in 2012.

Carolyn joined ANZ in 2010 as a portfolio analyst. After moving to Auckland, she joined Fisher and Paykel Finance as credit policy manager, where she worked with industry professionals on Comprehensive Credit Reporting (the Principles of Reciprosity and Data Requirements). Carolyn joined Latitude Financial Services as risk manager collections and recoveries (A&NZ). In 2018 Carolyn joined start-up ADEPT Decisions as head of Analytical Development, developing internal analytics capabilities and working with clients such as MTN and MiWay insurance.

Carolyn holds a BSc(Hons) from the University of Cape Town and a Master of Analytics (Business) from Massey University, New Zealand.

Outside work, Carolyn spends time with her wonderful, patient and supportive husband and two encouraging teenage daughters. You may also find her walking the beach in wild weather, playing underwater hockey or socialising with some of the wonderful people she's met since moving to New Zealand.

Find out more about Carolyn at
www.carolynrohm.com

Book a no obligation
30-minute free Discovery Call

Or mail Carolyn at carolyn@carolynrohm.com

Connect on LinkedIn: https://www.linkedin.com/in/carolynrohm/

Glossary

Active account

An active account has a balance outstanding or a charge or payment activity within a specified time, typically the previous 12 months.

Adverse selection

The inability to attract good customers results in a lower than expected proportion of good accounts and a higher than expected proportion of bad accounts. We acquire bad customers more easily than good customers. This can be driven by poor process, poor targeting or a weak offering.

Application (form, for credit)

A credit application is typically made by completing an application form, either online or via an app. It asks for sufficient information and permissions to enable a lender to make a lending decision. Application forms vary in length and complexity based on product and lender.

Application score

A number, typically between 0 and 1000 designed to rank order applications for credit. Applications are commonly ranked based on risk.

Auths/authorisation

The process whereby individual transactions, such as credit card purchases, are approved by the lender. Auths are typically highly automated, and only in exceptional circumstances will the customer be asked to call the lender for confirmation.

Bad rate

The ratio, often expressed as a percentage, of the number of bad accounts or outstanding balances relative to the total number of (active) accounts or outstanding balances.

Bads

A bad account is typically defined as an account that is frequently or severely delinquent.

Balance outstanding

The total principal and any current or past due interest on an account at any time. This is also known as the balance or receivables.

Behaviour score

A score, typically a number between 0 and 1000, that ranks existing accounts based on risk. Behaviour scores typically use internal information to score the account. High scores typically indicate lower risk, whereas low scores indicate higher risk.

Characteristic

A variable used to calculate the score.

Charge-off

Most lenders charge-off accounts that have missed a predetermined number of payments. This occurs when the lender deems the balance outstanding on the account uncollectable.

Credit bureau

A company that collects, files and reports information relating to the credit balances (some jurisdictions), repayment history and enquiry information of individuals and makes it available to banks, finance companies, etc. Typically, these individual pieces of information are summarised in a credit bureau score.

Credit cycle

This cycle involves borrowers' ease of access to credit based on economic expansion or contraction. Access to credit is typically more difficult during times of contraction and easier during times of expansion.

Credit risk life cycle

The credit risk life cycle is centred around the key elements of managing consumer credit products, namely account originations and account management, including credit limit management, transaction authorisation and collections or arrears management.

Credit history

This is an individual's current and past performance on their accounts. The information can be sourced from a credit provider's records or a credit bureau.

Credit score/scoring

A generic term for application, behaviour or credit bureau scoring. The scoring process rank orders applications or accounts based on the odds that they will perform in a specified way. Risk is typically used to rank order applications or accounts.

Cross-sell

Offering new or additional products to existing customers.

Cure

This is the term used to describe an account that was in arrears, and has made sufficient payment to ensure that the account is now up-to-date (UTD) and has no balance in arrears.

Cure rate

This is the percentage of accounts (or balances) that were in arrears last month and have made sufficient payment to meet the cure definition this month. It is expressed as a percentage of the total number of accounts or balances at a specific level of arrears last month.

Cut-off score

This is a score (calculated by a scoring system). One action is applied to applications or accounts with a higher score, while a different action is applied to those with a lower score.

Days past due (DPD)

This is the number of days after the payment due date that the account remains unpaid. It is typically used in personal loans. DPD are often grouped into buckets so that the DPD aligns with delinquency, often used to describe cards or revolving products. 1-29 DPD aligns with one cycle delinquent, which means that the account is one payment in arrears. 30-59 DPD aligns with two cycles delinquent, which means that the account is two payments in arrears, etc.

Decline overrides

Also known as low-side overrides. This is a decision to override the system-recommended decision to decline the applicant, and approve them instead.

Delinquency (Delq)

This describes the state of the account when the contractual amount due on an account has not been paid.

Demographic data

Demographic data is the term used to describe data that pertains to an individual and tends to remain static or only change slowly over time. Examples include age, address, phone number, education, etc.

Exploratory data analysis (EDA)

This is an essential and critical part of the initial investigation into data. It is used to spot patterns and anomalies, and test hypotheses and check assumptions. It is typically conducted using a combination of descriptive analysis and visualisations.

Good/bad odds (GBOdds)

The ratio of good to bad accounts or balances in a population.

Mill

This term describes an account that was at a specific level of arrears last month, and has made sufficient payment to ensure the account is still at that level of arrears this month.

Mill rate

This is the percentage of accounts or balances that meet the 'mill' definition, expressed as a percentage of all the accounts or balances at that level of arrears last month.

Minimum amount due

This is the minimum monthly payment of principal and interest contractually required to be paid to avoid becoming delinquent.

Odds

The likelihood of a specific event occurring.

Operational negation

This occurs when operational teams override the credit risk strategy and undo or contradict the actions in the strategy. This is often the result of poor communication and the operational teams being held accountable for results, and not buying into the credit risk strategy developed to support those outcomes.

Partial payment

A payment that is less than the amount contractually due.

Receivables

The total principal and any current or past due interest that remains to be paid on an account at any point in time. This is also known as the balance or balance outstanding.

Recoveries

Payments made to an account after it has been charged-off.

Roll

This term is used to describe an account that was at a specific level of arrears last month, and has not made sufficient payment. This month the account is more delinquent than it was last month.

Roll rate

This is the percentage of accounts or balances that meet the 'roll' definition, expressed as a percentage of all the accounts or balances at that level of arrears last month.

Scorecard

The individual characteristics and attributes and associated weights used in calculating a score.

Underwrite

The process of reviewing, analysing and deciding whether to approve, reject or request more information on an application. This is a manual process. Changes to credit risk policy rules can impact the volume of applications underwriters have to review and decide manually.

Up-to-date (UTD)

Accounts are described as being up-to-date (UTD) when there are no arrears on the account and they are in good order.

Verification

The process of verifying that the customer is who they say they are and that the information supplied within the application form or process is accurate.

Vintage

Sometimes known as a cohort; this is a block of accounts acquired during the same period of time under standard terms and conditions. Typically, vintages are used to analyse performance.

References

1. Corporate Finance Institute. (n.d.). *Purpose of Credit Risk Analysis*. https://corporatefinanceinstitute.com/resources/knowledge/credit/purpose-of-credit-risk-analysis/

2. ibid

3. *Credit Risk*. (n.d.). Graydon. https://graydon.co.uk/resources/wiki/credit-risk

4. uniPoint. *3 Important Aspects Of Data Importing | uniPoint Software Inc.* (n.d.). uniPoint Software Inc. https://www.unipointsoftware.com/blog/data-importing/3-importantaspects-of-data-importing

5. Baesens, B., Rösch, D., & Scheule, H. (2016). *Credit Risk Analytics*. John Wiley & Sons, Inc. https://doi.org/10.1002/9781119449560

6. Vanawat, N. (2021, August 12). *How To Perform Exploratory Data Analysis - A Guide for Beginners*. Analytics Vidhya. https://www.analyticsvidhya.com/blog/2021/08/how-to-perform-exploratory-data-analysis-a-guide-for-beginners/

7. Baesens, B., Rösch, D., & Scheule, H. (2016). *Credit Risk Analytics*. John Wiley & Sons, Inc. https://doi.org/10.1002/9781119449560

8.   Campuslabs. *Types of Descriptive Statistics*. https://
     baselinesupport.campuslabs.com/hc/en-us/
     articles/204305665-Types-of-Descriptive-Statistics

9.   Contributors to Wikimedia projects. (2002, February 5).
     Correlation does not imply causation - Wikipedia. Wikipedia,
     the free encyclopedia. https://en.wikipedia.org/wiki/
     Correlation_does_not_imply_causation

10. Cote, C. (2021, March 16). *5 Principles of Data Ethics for
     Business*. Business Insights Blog. https://online.hbs.edu/blog/
     post/data-ethics

11. Floridi, L., and Taddeo, M. (2016). What is data ethics?.
     *Philosophical Transactions of the Royal Society A:
     Mathematical, Physical and Engineering Sciences*,
     374(2083), p.20160360.

12. *What Is Data Ethics? | Cognizant*. (n.d.). Intuition durch
     Technologie – Einsicht in Echtzeit | Cognizant Deutschland.
     https://www.cognizant.com/us/en/glossary/data-ethics

13. Hayes, A. (2009, February 24). *How Credit Cycles Work*.
     Investopedia. https://www.investopedia.com/terms/c/credit-
     cycle.asp

14. ibid

15. Lawrence, D. (2002). *Managing a consumer lending
     business*. New York: Solomon Lawrence Partners.

16. Dun & Bradstreet. (n.d.). *Understanding Credit Scorecards*.
     ebook https://www.dnb.com/content/dam/english/business-
     trends/business-credit-scorecard-ebook.pdf

17. *What is a Propensity Score? | checkmyfile.* (n.d.). Multi Agency Credit Report | Free for 30 Days | checkmyfile. https://www.checkmyfile.com/jargon/propensity-score.htm

18. Liu, S. (2018, April 7). *Credit Scoring - Scorecard Development Process.* Medium.com. https://medium.com/@yanhuiliu104/credit-scoring-scorecard-development-process-8554c3492b2b

19. Contributors to Wikimedia projects. (2003, September 1). *Adverse selection - Wikipedia.* Wikipedia, the free encyclopedia. https://en.wikipedia.org/wiki/Adverse_selection

20. New Zealand Government. (n.d.). *Check your own credit record.* https://www.govt.nz/browse/consumer-rights-and-complaints/debt-and-credit-records/check-your-own-credit-report/

21. *CCR.* (n.d.). Equifax New Zealand. https://www.equifax.co.nz/business-enterprise/products/ccr

22. The Investopedia Team. (2007, May 20). *Credit Scoring.* Investopedia. https://www.investopedia.com/terms/c/credit_scoring.asp

23. Retail Credit Association of New Zealand Inc. *Data Standards.* https://rcanz.org.nz/resources/

24. Bhalla, D. (n.d.). *Credit Risk: Vintage Analysis.* ListenData. https://www.listendata.com/2019/09/credit-risk-vintage-analysis.html

25. Tian, F. (2021). *Unsecured Lending Risk Management*. Green Wheat Publishing.

26. Sanagapati, P. (2020, September 6). *Ensemble Learning Techniques Tutorial*. Kaggle: Your Machine Learning and Data Science Community. https://www.kaggle.com/code/pavansanagapati/ensemble-learning-techniques-tutorial?scriptVersionId=35569112

27. Callies, D., & Sharon, G. (n.d.). IBM - Deutschland IBM. https://www.ibm.com/garage/method/practices/think/what-if-analysis/

28. Zak, P. (2013, April 7). *Measurement Myopia*. Drucker Institute. https://www.drucker.institute/thedx/measurement-myopia/

29. Contributors to Wikimedia projects. (2002, July 7). *Markov chain - Wikipedia*. Wikipedia, the free encyclopedia. https://en.wikipedia.org/wiki/Markov_chain

30. Plesser, H. E. (2018, January 18). *Reproducibility vs. Replicability: A Brief History of a Confused Terminology*. PubMed Central (PMC). https://www.ncbi.nlm.nih.gov/pmc/articles/PMC5778115/

31. Ganti, A. (2007, May 10). *Central Limit Theorem (CLT): Definition and Key Characteristics*. Investopedia. https://www.investopedia.com/terms/c/central_limit_theorem.asp

Index